Ethnicity
MATTERS

Joseph L. DeVitis & Linda Irwin-DeVitis
GENERAL EDITORS

Vol. 39

PETER LANG
New York • Washington, D.C./Baltimore • Bern
Frankfurt am Main • Berlin • Brussels • Vienna • Oxford

Ethnicity
MATTERS

RETHINKING HOW BLACK, HISPANIC,
& INDIAN STUDENTS PREPARE FOR
& SUCCEED IN COLLEGE

MARYJO BENTON LEE, EDITOR

PETER LANG
New York • Washington, D.C./Baltimore • Bern
Frankfurt am Main • Berlin • Brussels • Vienna • Oxford

Library of Congress Cataloging-in-Publication Data

Ethnicity matters: rethinking how Black, Hispanic, and Indian students
prepare for and succeed in college / edited by MaryJo Benton Lee.
p. cm. — (Adolescent cultures, school, and society; v. 39)
Includes bibliographical references and index.
1. Minorities—Education (Higher)—United States. 2. College preparation
programs—United States. I. Lee, MaryJo Benton. II. Series:
Adolescent cultures, school & society; v. 39.
LC3731.E875   378.1'9829—dc22   2005022538
ISBN 0-8204-7602-1
ISSN 1091-1464

Bibliographic information published by **Die Deutsche Bibliothek**.
Die Deutsche Bibliothek lists this publication in the "Deutsche
Nationalbibliografie"; detailed bibliographic data is available
on the Internet at http://dnb.ddb.de/.

The paper in this book meets the guidelines for permanence and durability
of the Committee on Production Guidelines for Book Longevity
of the Council of Library Resources.

© 2006 Peter Lang Publishing, Inc., New York
29 Broadway, New York, NY 10006
www.peterlang.com

Printed in the United States of America

This book is dedicated to

Enrique (Henry) T. Trueba

1931–2004

Teacher
Researcher
Author
Scholar

Best known for his tireless advocacy of learning opportunities
for those in greatest need.

He is loved by hundreds of students and colleagues
with whom he worked in trying to make the world
a better place through education.

What about you, boy?

What about you, boy?
Is your work coming along?
Are you still making candles
Against darkness and wrong?
The whole thing is to blast.
Blast and blast again. To fill the Black
With songs, poems, temples, paintings,
Anything at all. Attack. Attack.
Open up and let go.
Even if it's only blowing. But blast.
And I say this loving my God.
Because we are all He has at last.
So what about it, boy?
Is your work going well?
Are you still lighting lamps
Against darkness and Hell?

Frederick Manfred
Winter Count
"The Old Black Silence," Part VI

Table of Contents

Foreword: Resilience and Ethnicity

The intuitive—and often biased—view of ethnic minorities is that they are handicapped and therefore less likely than mainstream people to achieve academically. This view ignores the experience of minority persons who strive all their lives to belong, to participate in the benefits of society and to improve the quality of their existence at any cost. Through their struggles, ethnic minorities often obtain a special social and cultural capital that permits them to pursue with a singular determination, energy and vision the achievement goals that seem unimaginable to mainstream people. The rich social and cultural capital obtained by minorities provides them with a unique resilience.

Resilience, as a concept based on empirical research, is not a simple stoic resistance to hardships. Resilience is neither the capacity to tolerate mental and physical pain nor the ability to suffer sleep or food deprivation. Resilience goes beyond unreasoned or unmotivated suffering of any kind.

There is in all resilience a clear element of endurance to difficult circumstances, but this endurance is rational. Resilience is motivated by ethical principles, noble causes and deep commitments, as discussed by Paulo Freire. Often reasons of delayed satisfaction explain resilience. In other words, resilience is part of a plan, of a strategy to sacrifice something in the present in order to obtain other compensating benefits in the future. *Resilience is a strategic and intelligent approach to endure any sufferings or difficulties for the sake of realizing specific goals, in the service of a worthwhile cause.*

Resilience is intimately related to self-identity. The most resilient individuals demonstrate an ability to use multiple identities. Resilient individuals from minority groups can code-switch and interact—with ethnic persons and white persons, with less educated community members and with highly trained educational leaders. This ability is based on their multicultural experiences, on their skills in various languages and on their ability to live in different worlds culturally and cognitively.

Resilient individuals understand the strategic value of playing different roles and of using different languages. They control their communicative skills by sending different messages to different audiences. They manipulate information using various possible frameworks of interpretation.

Resilience can be of many different types—physical or mental, temporary or final, expressed through action or through silence. Resilience is a quality of the spirit, consciously developed and clearly expressed. Resilience can be manifested in a number of different circumstances of life.

During a trip to China in 1992, we were talking to Miao nationality students at the Central University for Nationalities in Beijing. (The Miao are a Chinese minority with a very low status and a history of oppression and prejudice; socialization to become good Miao peasants was not the best preparation to become good university students.) These Miao university students were miles and miles away from their homes. They had left their Miao language school to enter the university in which Mandarin was the language of instruction. They lacked money for food. They hadn't seen their parents or family in maybe two years. Still they used to say things like, "I'm just a farm boy, but I want to make my parents proud of me."

What I learned from that hit me again going back to the Lower Rio Grande Valley in South Texas in 2001. I was teaching in the doctoral program of the University of Texas, Pan American. It was the first day of class. I began by asking the students why they got into teaching. One of the students, Sylvia, was a 45-year-old elementary school teacher from Laredo. She said:

> Let me tell you a story that explains it. I was a young teacher. I hardly made it to the certification. During the winter I am in this class with 30 kids. I am ready to start. I am complaining about the weather. It's too cold. I have this coat. I paid good money for it. I'm there standing up, and the door opens, and there is a kid running. I look at the kid, and he has big shoes, probably his father's shoes. His pants are tied up on top with a string, cut and rolled

because they are too big. And the T-shirt in that winter! It is transparent they had washed it so many times. It is a big one. He is running with his books. "Teacher, teacher what are we going to learn today?" he says in Spanish with a big smile. I saw that kid, and I said "I want to work with kids like these."

The specific agencies that lead to resilience and, in turn, to academic achievement are found within the family and community settings. It is the family and the community that give individuals their self-identity and motivation to excel.

Academic success for students of color depends upon the *integration* of the culture of the home and the culture of the school. This volume describes four programs that do just that. The authors who describe their programs share a profound commitment to intellectual work, a full engagement in action research and a serious decision to impact the lives of the young. These commitments have brought us together and have given us a chance to share our lives.

Enrique (Henry) T. Trueba
Ruben E. Hinojosa Regents Professor Emeritus
University of Texas, Austin

Sections of the foreword are from a keynote address delivered by Dr. Trueba at a conference titled "Ethnicity Matters—Rethinking How Black, Hispanic and Indian Students Prepare for and Succeed in College," hosted by South Dakota State University, October 18–19, 2002, Brookings, South Dakota.

Acknowledgments

Nothing benefits learning more than being associated with the right people.

The Confucian scholar Xunzi wrote those words 2200 years ago, and they are still true today. It has been my good fortune to have been associated with the right people throughout my life and especially throughout the 20 years I have worked at South Dakota State University (SDSU). The completion of *Ethnicity Matters* would not have been possible without these people.

First, I would like to thank SDSU, especially Provost and Vice President for Academic Affairs Carol J. Peterson, Executive Vice President for Administration Michael P. Reger, and Professor Emeritus and Director of Diversity Allen Branum, for their support of the working conference, "Ethnicity Matters—Rethinking How Black, Hispanic and Indian Students Prepare for and Succeed in College," held at SDSU in October 2002. This book grew out of that conference. Financial support was provided by SDSU and its Office for Diversity Enhancement.

A steering committee, composed of faculty and staff from throughout the university, labored for months to plan and implement the conference. These individuals are treasured colleagues who have committed their lives to working for and with students of color in higher education: Allen Branum; C.D. Douglas, executive director of Multicultural Affairs; Ruth Harper, professor of Counseling and Human Resource Development; Valerian Three Irons, Service-Learning associate; and Jeff Maras, former director of TRiO Student Support Services. I deeply appreciate them for believing in the idea behind the conference and for working hard to bring it to fruition.

The SDSU College of Engineering, led by Dean Lewis Brown and Assistant Dean Richard Reid, was a key sponsor of the Ethnicity Matters conference and thus of this book. As diversity coordinator for the College of Engineering, much of my work in the months preceding October 2002 was devoted to the conference. The support of Kevin Dalsted, director of the Engineering Resource Center (ERC), where my office is housed, and Kim Steineke, ERC secretary, was also crucial to the success of this project. Kim is a tireless colleague whose devotion to detail and concern for diversity benefited immensely the conference and later the book. I thank all of these friends for their help in the organization of the conference and for their advocacy on behalf of students of color.

I would also like to recognize the work of Distinguished Professor of English Charles L. Woodard. For the past 30 years he has been the conscience of SDSU. By example, he has taught an entire generation of younger scholars how to speak out against inequality in education and how to lead the way toward equal access for all. We are forever in his debt.

The Ethnicity Matters conference brought to the campus of SDSU a distinguished group of educators and activists, individuals who have been deeply involved throughout their careers with issues of ethnic identity, empowerment processes and educational reform. They are Julia E. Colyar, assistant professor of Educational Administration and Higher Education at Southern Illinois University Carbondale (speaking on the Neighborhood Academic Initiative); Tim Nichols, assistant director of academic programs at SDSU's College of Agriculture, and Laurie Stenberg Nichols, dean of SDSU's College of Family and Consumer Sciences (speaking on 2+2+2); Derek Vergara, then executive director, and Keisha Bentley, cross-cultural programs director, of the Institute for Multicultural Research and Campus Diversity at the University of La Verne (speaking on the First Generation Student Success Program); and Diane Gillespie, professor and associate director of Interdisciplinary Arts and Sciences at The University of Washington, Bothell, and Reshell Ray, project director for Critical Moments and assistant director of student involvement at University of Nebraska-Lincoln (speaking on Critical Moments). I thank them for their willingness to share their stories, first orally with conference attendees at SDSU and later in writing through their *Ethnicity Matters* chapters.

Those who spoke and wrote about 2+2+2, First Generation Student

Success Program and Critical Moments are also the creators of these innovative and effective programs that have been serving students of color at their respective universities for the past ten years. I have long been following the work of these individuals from afar, learning from their challenges and their successes. It is an honor for me to write this book with them.

We owe a deep debt of gratitude to Len Hightower, vice president for enrollment management and director of strategic planning at Pacific University in Oregon; to Gillies Malnarich, co-director of The Washington Center for Improving the Quality of Undergraduate Education at The Evergreen State College; and to Dr. George Woods, of the Department of Psychiatry at the Morehouse School of Medicine and of the Department of Educational Leadership and Public Policy at California State University, Sacramento. Len co-authored with Derek Chapter Four on the First Generation Student Success Program, and Gillies and George co-authored with Diane Chapter Five on Critical Moments. Len, Gillies and George graciously agreed to join our Ethnicity Matters team, as the project moved from conference to book. Without their contributions, this book would never have been completed.

Good scholarship, by necessity, must build on the work of others. In writing Chapters One and Six, I relied heavily on work in the areas of equity and access by William G. Tierney. Dr. Tierney is director of the Center for Higher Education Policy Analysis and Wilbur-Kieffer Professor of Higher Education at the Rossier School of Education at the University of Southern California. Inspiration also came from a number of other individuals, who have managed over the course of a lifetime to combine scholarship with activism: Francisco J. Guajardo and Miguel A. Guajardo of the Llano Grande Center for Research and Development in Edcouch, Texas; Hugh Mehan of the Achievement Via Individual Determination (AVID) program in San Diego, California; and George Farkas, creator of the Reading One-One program in Dallas, Texas, and now professor of sociology at The Pennsylvania State University. These scholar-activists serve as my daily role models, examples of all I aspire to be. I owe them my sincere thanks.

My work as coordinator of the SDSU-Flandreau Indian School (FIS) Success Academy continues to inform my research and enrich my life. The dedication of the FIS staff—led by Superintendent Betty Belkham, Principal Stuart Zephier and Vice Principal Sandra Koester—to the education of American Indian students is enormous. The Success Academy Scholars, who graduate from FIS and attend SDSU, are my own personal heroes and heroines, because of their ability to survive and thrive in the face of obstacles. I thank all my close friends at FIS—faculty, staff, administrators and students—for what you continue to teach me about ethnicity and education.

My understanding of the relationship between ethnic identity and academic achievement was further enhanced by the work of Daphna Oyserman of the University of Michigan and by the work of Carolyn R. Hodges and Olga M. Welch, both of the University of Tennessee-Knoxville. I am also indebted to Tara J. Yosso of the University of California, Santa Barbara, for her development of the concept of community cultural wealth. The research of these four scholars forms the basis for the model, "How Students of Color Succeed," presented in Chapter Six.

SDSU was an extremely supportive environment in which to work on the editing of this volume. The staff at the Hilton M. Briggs Library spent endless hours answering my questions and directing me to resources. My sincere thanks go to reference librarians Clark Hallman, David Alexander, Mary Kraljic, Vickie Mix and Laura Wight, and also to Mary Caspers-Graper, acquisitions librarian; Elizabeth Fox, circulation librarian; and Stephen Van Buren, archivist. Mary Lou Berry and Ellen Berg of the interlibrary loan staff were godsends, tracking down hundreds of articles and books on ethnicity and education from around the country. SDSU graphic designer Virginia Coudron created the original Ethnicity Matters logo, and Graphic Design major Teresa Brown designed the model in Chapter Six, two more invaluable contributions to the project.

The manuscript benefited from the careful editing done first by Professor Ruth Harper of SDSU's Department of Counseling and Human Resource Development and Professor Diane Kayongo-Male of SDSU's Department of Rural Sociology; next by Joseph L. DeVitis and Linda Irwin-DeVitis of Georgia College and State University; and finally by Christopher S. Myers and Bernadette Shade of Peter Lang Publishing.

I thank Freya Manfred for permission to reprint "What about you, boy?" from her father Frederick Manfred's book *Winter Count* (second edition), "The Old Black Silence," Part VI. The poem speaks to me and, I believe, to all for whom ethnicity matters.

In acknowledging my gratitude for the opportunity to write this book, I conclude with the question, "Why *does* ethnicity matter to me?" I believe the answer rests with five people. To them I owe my deepest thanks.

My parents, Catherine W. Benton (1920–) and George E. Benton (1916–2005) have always been my best teachers. They truly believed in equity and justice for all and tried to teach me to do the same.

My SDSU colleague, writing partner and dear friend, Professor Diane Kayongo-Male, first suggested the idea for *Ethnicity Matters* four years ago, and since then has helped work in every way toward the book's completion. As a scholar of the African family, Diane exemplifies the highest calling of the sociologist—to better understand and improve the human condition.

Professor Emeritus Richard W. Lee, my husband and my most cherished friend, has joyfully shared in each moment of the Ethnicity Matters process, including, very importantly, the final step of turning computer-generated words into a finished book. As head of SDSU's Department of Journalism and Mass Communication for 24 years, Dick was a national leader among those working to increase the number of Native Americans in the media. I am forever grateful for his vision, his intellect, his encouragement and his labor, all so generously invested in me and in this book's completion.

Dr. Enrique (Henry) T. Trueba (1931–2004) came to the United States from Mexico, acquired English as a second language and spent a lifetime advocating for immigrant students. He is loved by hundreds of students and colleagues, including those of us whose lives he touched as keynote speaker at the Ethnicity Matters conference at SDSU. By dedicating this book to Henry, we dedicate our lives to carrying on the work he began—making education accessible to *all* peoples, that they might be empowered to assume productive roles in an equitable society.

1
Ethnicity Matters

MaryJo Benton Lee

Fifty years have passed since the landmark *Brown v. Board of Education* decision by the Supreme Court, the decision that formally ended legal school segregation in the United States. The anniversary of *Brown v. Board of Education* provides an opportunity to pause and reflect on how students of color—in our families, in our communities, in our schools and in our universities—are doing relative to college preparation, admission and retention. Some facts to consider:

• High school completion rates for black, Hispanic and Indian students are still substantially below those of whites and Asian Americans.
• The trend away from need-based financial aid, coupled with rising fees at public universities, means that higher education is becoming affordable primarily to families of the middle and upper class. Conversely, there has been a rapid growth in merit aid, as institutions compete for the "best" students, so defined by high grades and test scores. Universities now garner favor based on the test scores of their entering students. This works against minority students who often come from low-income communities with failing schools.
• Low-income and minority students who do gain admittance to universities often require educational support programs in order to succeed in college. Tutoring, mentoring and advising services are either nonexistent, understaffed or underfunded at most higher

education institutions. Meanwhile, policymakers insist that re-mediation should occur at the K–12 level in schools funded by an antiquated property tax system.

• Attacks on affirmative action, which started in California and Texas, have now spread to other states as well. Minority college enrollment in both California and Texas declined after courts declared affirmative action plans unconstitutional. While some states have banned bilingual education programs, others states have barred undocumented aliens from attending public institutions. Foes of affirmative action have yet to propose any viable alternatives. The result has been closing the doors of higher education to many students of color and allowing the universities they might have attended to remain predominantly white.

• Finally, and not surprisingly, black, Hispanic and Indian students continue to trail considerably behind whites and Asian Americans in rates of four-year college completion.

These findings are from *Reflections on 20 Years of Minorities in Higher Education and the ACE Annual Status Report* (American Council on Education 2004). The *Annual Status Report* published by the American Council on Education (ACE) is considered the publication of record, documenting the progress of minorities from high school through graduate education. The first ACE status report, prepared in 1982, described some disturbing trends about minority high school completion and college graduation rates, trends that sadly still hold true today.

During the past 20 years, myriad programs have begun to help more minority youth get into, and graduate from, college. As William Tierney (2000) suggests, many traditional minority college preparation and retention programs focus on the individual. They suggest that being a member of a minority group is a handicap in the pursuit of higher education. One outcome of these traditional programs is often to encourage minority students to abandon ties with family, peers and community. These ties are viewed, in the best case, as not being beneficial to one's success in education, and, in the worst case, as being outright harmful to academic achievement. Traditional programs for minority students frequently attempt to re-form these individuals into persons who can survive and prevail in the existing, predominantly white, educational system. These programs stress student assimilation into mainstream culture as the sure route to academic success.

We need look no farther than the ACE data already discussed to see that these traditional approaches to minority college student preparation and retention, by and large, do not work. Clearly, educators need to rethink how they work with students of color.

Ethnicity Matters—Rethinking How Black, Hispanic and Indian Students Prepare for and Succeed in College focuses on four innovative programs that are highly effective in preparing students from underrepresented groups for college and in supporting these students through baccalaureate degree completion. These four model programs serve students from those ethnic groups that face the most serious problems of underrepresentation in American higher education—African Americans, Latino/as and American Indians. What sets these four programs apart from many other minority college preparation and retention efforts is that they are built on this proposition: *Ethnic identity can play an empowering role in academic achievement.*

The remainder of Chapter One will look at this proposition from three perspectives—the practical, the theoretical and the personal. First, from a practical standpoint, the four model programs that make ethnic identity central to academic success will be described. In the next section, the theoretical orientation of the book will be discussed, as well as the literature relevant to ethnic identity and educational achievement. Finally, since a book is better understood when the readers know something about the writer, Chapter One will conclude with some remarks about the personal journey that led me to edit a book on ethnicity, education and empowerment.

The Practical

Four Model Programs

The four model programs that make ethnic identity central to educational success are the Neighborhood Academic Initiative (NAI) in south central Los Angeles, 2+2+2 at South Dakota State University (SDSU), the First Generation Student Success Program (FGSSP) at the University of La Verne in Southern California and Critical Moments, which operates at a number of universities nationwide.

Neighborhood Academic Initiative. Chapter Two describes NAI. NAI involves middle school and high school students, primarily black and Hispanic, from south central Los Angeles. All NAI participants are called "Scholars" to emphasize their academic potential (Tierney 2000:225). NAI scholars attend accelerated English and math classes at the University of Southern California (USC), receiving academic credit from their respective home schools. NAI Scholars also attend Saturday Academy, a weekly four-hour workshop covering communication, math, science, information technology and college entrance exam preparation skills. NAI Scholars who meet admission requirements receive four-and-one-half–year tuition scholarships to USC.

NAI makes the negotiation of identity central to educational success. A clear message is sent to NAI Scholars that they do not have to abandon their ethnic identities to achieve in school. Teachers and administrators in the program are often African American or Hispanic (Tierney 2000:229). They work closely with the students' families and communities toward a common goal—the students' completion of high school and enrollment in college.

2+2+2. Chapter Three covers the 2+2+2 program. It is a collaborative effort among reservation high schools, tribal colleges and SDSU to help more American Indians complete baccalaureate degrees in agricultural, biological, family and consumer sciences. The 2+2+2 graduates are prepared to work toward solving some of the most pressing challenges facing tribal people today—economic development, land and resource management, and family and community well-being. Important components of the 2+2+2 project are articulation agreements, faculty development, curriculum revision, student support, distance education and experiential learning.

The attrition rate for American Indian students in postsecondary education greatly exceeds that of non-Indian students. For many American Indians, completing a college degree means separation from their tribal communities and extended families. The 2+2+2 program counters this obstacle to student success by building bridges between tribal and nontribal entities. These bridges ensure the easy movement of American Indian students between on- and off-reservation institutions—and toward college degree completion.

First Generation Student Success Program. Chapter Four outlines FGSSP at the University of La Verne in Southern California. FGSSP is a comprehensive program for first generation college students and their families. More than half of the University of La Verne's students are minorities, with the largest number (32 percent) being Latino/a. Consequently, a majority of the FGSSP participants are Latino/a.

Nationwide, students whose parents do not have college degrees are almost twice as likely to drop out of college as those whose parents have college degrees. First generation college students, particularly those from minority groups, often face culturally based conflicts between the demands of family and the demands of college. For example, traditional Latino/a families frequently expect their daughters to help with child care and housework, even after they start college. Students who face such conflicts are at great risk of dropping out. FGSSP works with students and families *together*, explaining college expectations and supports available to ensure academic success for program participants. Orientation sessions before college and continuing workshops throughout the academic year are designed for students *and* families. Mentoring and scholarships are also provided for FGSSP students.

Critical Moments. Chapter Five discusses Critical Moments, a retention, awareness and change project for students of color and the institutions they attend. Critical Moments has been implemented at the University of Nebraska-Lincoln and at four colleges in Washington State. Critical Moments prepares students, faculty and administrators to respond proactively to campus events that involve race, gender, class and other differences. A multicultural team of case writers interviews underrepresented students. Each interview focuses on an experience that caused the student to think about dropping out of college, that is, a "critical moment." These experiences then become the basis of small-group class discussions involving faculty, students of color and white students. Together they develop critical-thinking skills, problem-solving strategies and communication tools that foster student success.

Critical Moments, in the words of its creators, "allows students to discuss the social construction of categories surrounding race…and the complex relationship between identity and experience." The program helps students of color assemble a survival kit of skills to deal effectively with critical moments when they occur. Students learn how to redefine problematic situations that affect academic achievement.

The Theoretical

Key Questions

  • Does a strong ethnic identity empower students of color to achieve academically?
  • If so, why do students who have strong ethnic identities tend to do well in school?
  • Furthermore, how could this knowledge be used to foster academic success for students of color?

These questions, and the answers to them, are central to understanding programs that help minority students prepare for and succeed in college. It is important to review the literature on minority students' success in education before discussing specific programs that help students of color do well in school.

Theory and practice must be inseparable. Thus, in this section, existing theory will be reviewed. Chapters Two through Five will illustrate ways in which this theory is applied. Chapter Six will present a new causal model, based on existing theory and current practice, which suggests the relationship between ethnic identity construction and minority student success in college preparation and retention programs.

Historical Background

Tinto's model of college student departure. Many traditional programs aimed at helping minority youth prepare for and succeed in college focus on the individual. These programs have been greatly influenced by the work of Vincent Tinto (1975, 1993). Tinto's highly acclaimed model of institutional departure attempts to explain student attrition from college.

Tinto (1993:113) calls his model "longitudinal and interactional." The model describes an individual student's decision to stay or depart from college as a process that occurs over time and is an interplay between characteristics of the student and characteristics of the institution. The model suggests that the students who complete degrees are those who become firmly integrated into the mainstream academic and social systems of the institutions they attend. This has particular significance for students of color, because it suggests that they bear the burden of changing their ethnic identities in order to fit into predominantly white institutions.

Interactionalist theories, like Tinto's, are linked to the assimilation/ acculturation perspectives prevalent in the late 1960s. As Laura Rendon, Romero Jalomo and Amaury Nora (2000) explain:

> It was believed that minority individuals were engaged in a self-perpetuating cycle of poverty and deprivation and that they could avoid societal alienation by becoming full absorbed (assimilated) or adapted (acculturated) into the dominant culture...During the 1970s and 1980s critics contested this perspective, citing problems such as the use of mainstream cultural norms as evaluative criteria, as well as the problematic assumption that minority group norms and cultural patterns were inferior, deviant, and self-destructive when compared to those of the majority culture. (P. 128)

Challenges to Tinto's model. Since the creation of the model nearly 30 years ago, Tinto has modified it, and now says that students of color, if they are to be retained, need supportive campus communities and inclusive university environments. Nevertheless, Tinto's model has been challenged by numerous researchers (Ogbu 1978; Rendon, Jalomo, and Nora 2000; Tierney 1993), who argue that the model is still firmly embedded in an assimilation/acculturation framework that is not valid to explain the experiences of nonwhite students.

Tinto's model of institutional departure is both an *individualistic* and a *functionalist model.* Tierney (2000:215) draws an analogy between Tinto's model of institutional departure (Tinto 1993) and Durkheim's idea of suicide (Durkheim 1951). Tinto focuses on the *individual* student who drops out; Durkheim focuses on the *individual* person who commits suicide. *Functionalists* view the larger society, beyond individual actors, as a working unit, with all parts interdependent and operating together for the social whole. Neither Tinto nor Durkheim critically examine the larger cultural context in which individual action occurs, the context that makes dropping out or committing suicide possible (Tierney 2000:215).

Traditional college preparation and retention programs, based on Tinto's model, treat minority students as if they are broken and in need of repair, Tierney (2000) maintains. The goal of such programs is to re-form minority students into people who can survive in the existing educational system. "Needed are new models that consider the key theoretical issues associated with the experiences of minority students in higher education," write Rendon, Jalomo, and Nora (2000:129).

Theoretical Orientation of *Ethnicity Matters*: Critical Pedagogy

The assertions of Tinto's critics are borne out by experience. Traditional minority college preparation and retention programs are simply not working. Minorities continue to trail significantly behind whites on key educational indicators like college participation and graduation rates (Harvey 2003:3). The time has come to turn Tinto on his head.

The four model programs discussed in this book grow out of an entirely different paradigm, one that is based upon theories of post-structuralism and notions of power presented by Michel Foucault (1983) and Pierre Bourdieu (1977). Based on the pioneering work of Brazilian educational philosopher Paulo Freire (1992, 2002), this paradigm is known as critical pedagogy. As defined by Barry Kanpol (1994), critical pedagogy:

views schools as inherently unequal places of knowledge distribution that
in a large part serve to divide the United States by race, class, and gender.
That is, different people divided by race, class, and gender receive and/or
are privileged to receive certain forms of educational knowledge, skills, and
curriculum in unequal ways. (Pp. 2–3)

The literature of critical pedagogy focuses on the transformative
power of education, both for students of color and for the institutions
they attend. Kanpol (1994:175) explains that critical pedagogy "is not
only about theoretical ideas. It is about living those ideas in our daily
lives and out of our workplace." For critical pedagogists, the line between theory and praxis is thin to nonexistent. For example, Tierney
(2000), one of the most articulate proponents of critical pedagogy
writing today, argues for a fundamental reorientation of the culture of
schooling:

Power's grasp has a direct relationship with the achievement that minority
students face in educational settings in general and postsecondary institutions in particular. That is, power relations already existent in the larger
society frequently get transformed in educational organizations as failures for
those who are on the margins...What I am suggesting is that...we develop
a framework which has the negotiation of *identity* in academe as central to
educational success. The *interactions* that students, teachers, parents, and
families have and how we approach the *definitions* of these interactions are
key to students' success. (Pp. 218–219)

Tierney believes that successful programs that increase minority
access to higher education are built upon the following key sociological
concepts.

Identity. Effective programs "affirm and honor individual identities"
(Tierney 2000:220). These programs "equip students with the necessary cultural capital to succeed within the system that exists" (Tierney
2000:218).

Interactions with reference groups. Effective programs "assume students
are a valuable resource to themselves and their families, communities,
and society" (Tierney 2000:223). Such programs strongly encourage the
family and the community to participate in their children's academic
progress. Individuals without college degrees or formal educational
backgrounds often have other kinds of knowledge and strength that
teachers do not; consequently, their participation is critical.

Definitions of academic success. In effective programs, parents and teachers work together to create a definition of the situation that "assumes success" (Tierney 2000:225). The students involved are expected to complete high school and graduate from college, and numerous structures are in place to ensure that they do. Effective programs acknowledge that discrimination exists, while simultaneously teaching students strategies to overcome it.

In short, the four innovative programs discussed in this book meet perfectly the criteria set out by Tierney. The model programs are all built upon the idea that ethnicity matters, that fostering a strong ethnic identity can help minority students achieve academically. Furthermore, all the programs involve systemic change on the part of higher education institutions to increase minority college access. This is a stark contradiction to the traditional approaches, based upon the Tinto model, which require students of color to integrate into existing educational systems.

Ethnic Identity and School Performance: Competing Explanations

A central question that must be addressed is why ethnic identity is at some times a resource and at other times an obstacle to academic achievement. In searching the literature of sociology, education, psychology and anthropology for the past 20 years, two types of explanations emerge concerning black, Hispanic and Indian students. These explanations are the notion of *blocked opportunities*, as articulated by Signithia Fordham and John Ogbu (1986), and the idea of *cultural differences*, as represented by the work of Enrique (Henry) T. Trueba (Trueba 2004; Trueba and Zou 1994; Trueba, Jacobs, and Kirton 1990). Numerous authors (Iber 1992; Kao, Tienda, and Schneider 1996; Taylor 1997) have identified these two explanations as the major and divergent themes in the literature of education and underrepresented minorities produced during the past 20 years.

Blocked opportunities explanation. Ogbu (1978), in his cultural ecological theory, identifies three types of minority groups:

- *autonomous minorities*, who are minorities in number only (like Jews and Mormons) and thus have educational parity with whites;
- *immigrant minorities*, who have moved into the society voluntarily to enhance their economic and political well-being, and may excel in school due to motivation and self-selection; and

• *castelike minorities,* who have been involuntarily incorporated into the United States and fare the worst scholastically because poverty and discrimination restrict their educational opportunities. Caste-like minorities in the United States include Chicanos, Puerto Ricans, Native Hawaiians, American Indians and African Americans. (Most of Ogbu's work has focused on African Americans.)

Ogbu's cultural ecological theory posits a keen awareness on the part of African Americans about their access to jobs, wages and benefits appropriate to their level of education. This leads African Americans to question the value of school achievement in the face of persistent discrimination. This also leads African Americans to falsely perceive they have limited academic ability. Questioning the value of academic achievement and their ability to achieve academically, African Americans then develop an identity that opposes that of white Americans, including behaviors and values associated with academic achievement (Taylor et al. 1994).

Fordham, using Ogbu's cultural ecological theory, has examined African American students' underachievement at a Washington, D.C., high school (Fordham 1988, 1996; Fordham and Ogbu 1986). Her findings indicate that the characteristics required for success in mainstream society contradict the students' identification and solidarity with black culture. Consequently, the black students' fear of being accused by their peers of "acting white" diminishes academic effort and leads to underachievement.

In essence, Fordham and Ogbu's work predicts an inverse relationship between ethnic identity and school performance. In other words, the stronger the ethnic identity, the weaker the school performance. For the past 20 years, the cultural ecological theory has been one of the dominant theories used to explain the black-white achievement gap. Consequently, the idea that black students continue to underperform in school because of their cultural opposition to "acting white" has been examined extensively (Ford et al. 1994).

Some studies clearly refute the theory (Chapell and Overton 2002; Hall 1998), while other studies (Arroyo and Zigler 1995; Taylor et al. 1994) offer mixed support. For example, work by Carmen Arroyo and Edward Zigler (1995) suggests that the behaviors and attitudes described by Fordham and Ogbu are not specific to African American students. Academically gifted students, both white and black, feel they must choose between fulfilling their academic goals and establishing relationships with peers.

"It would be useful if future research addressed the conditions under which avoidance of acting white is most likely to occur," write David Bergin and Helen Cooks (2002:113). For example, A. A. Akom (2003) finds that young female members of the Nation of Islam, because of religious tenets, develop a "black achievement ideology" that results in academic success.

Erin Horvat and Kristine Lewis (2003) note that, in some urban high schools in California, black students are able to "manage" their academic success by downplaying accomplishments with some peers and sharing accomplishments with other peers. These students are able to both sustain an authentic black identity and achieve academically.

Still other researchers, working in a system of predominantly white elite independent schools in Maryland, observe the operation of informal peer networks of African American students (Datnow and Cooper 1997). The networks "support these students' academic success" and "create opportunities for them to reaffirm their racial identities." Amanda Datnow and Robert Cooper (1997:56) conclude that "the dynamics and ideologies of African American peer groups are more complex than prior research has suggested."

Cultural differences explanation. A number of scholars, including Trueba (1988), take issue with the blocked opportunities explanation, in part because it ignores those minority students who *do* succeed in school. Trueba says that explanations like Ogbu's stereotype minorities because they are overly deterministic and do not allow for human agency.

For Trueba (Trueba 2004; Trueba and Zou 1994; Trueba, Jacobs, and Kirton 1990), academic failure is not caused by socioeconomic factors that lead to a culture of resistance. Rather, academic failure is tied to a discontinuity between the culture of the home and the culture of the school (Trueba 1988). Minority children may perform poorly in school because schooling promotes middle-class, majority-culture values. Put another way, failure is due to culturally incongruent exchanges between minority students and the schools they attend.

Like Ogbu, Trueba is an educational ethnographer. Throughout his long career, Trueba's writing has centered around issues of race, ethnicity and adaptation. His most recent works have focused on Hmong children in California (Trueba, Jacobs, and Kirton 1990), Miao people (the ancestors of the Hmong) in China (Trueba and Zou 1994) and Latino/a immigrants and transnationals in Texas (Trueba 2004).

Trueba sees a strong ethnic identity as empowering minority students to succeed in school. Trueba believes there is a positive correlation between ethnic identity and school performance. In other words, the stronger the ethnic identity, the stronger the school performance.

A key concept for Trueba (2004:160) is "resiliency," which he defines as "a strategic approach to endure any sufferings or difficulties for the sake of realizing specific goals in the service of a worthwhile cause." One example from Trueba's prolific research captures the concept of resiliency and its outcome—academic achievement. Trueba and his then doctoral student Yali Zou in 1992 traveled to the People's Republic of China to study Miao students. The Miao are the fourth largest ethnic minority group in China. (The Miao are also the ancestors of the Hmong people living in California, who Trueba had studied earlier in his career.) Throughout Chinese history, the Miao have experienced significant levels of poverty and discrimination, and this has led to serious underachievement in school. The proportion of Miao youth going on to higher education is substantially lower than that of the majority (Han) youth.

In their research at the Central Institute for Nationalities in Beijing and at the Guizhou Institute for Nationalities in Guiyang, Trueba and Zou (1994) found numerous Miao students who had overcome almost insurmountable odds in order to achieve their educational and career goals. The very fact of being a Miao person, of belonging to a Miao family and of coming from a Miao community seemed to enable these students to function effectively in a second culture using a language other than their native one.

To explain their findings, that is, to explain academic success among minority students where failure might be expected, Trueba and Zou developed a theory of social identification and achievement motivation. Three propositions in the theory are outlined below.

- *Proposition one—home language and culture.* Ethnic language and culture play an important mediating role in the academic achievement of minority students. Ethnic students who are firmly grounded in their home languages are able to maintain relationships with their families, even when vast distances separate them. Knowledge of home languages and cultures allows minority students "to retain a strong self-concept and affiliation to the larger ethnic group, and thus to draw on this affiliation for an increased motivation to achieve academically" (Trueba and Zou 1994:131).
- *Proposition two—strong ethnic identity.* A strong ethnic identity empowers minority students, as they, in some cases, struggle to

master a second language and, in other cases, acquire the social skills necessary to survive in new learning environments (Trueba and Zou 1994:131). This proposition grows out of Freire's notion of "conscientization," the process through which oppressed people realize that their cultural values are legitimate and worth maintaining (Freire 2002).

• *Proposition three—sense of obligation and responsibility.* In the case of ethnic minority students in China, "their willingness to suffer pain and deprivation, to delay gratification and rewards, and to pursue a long and arduous course of intellectual development becomes an opportunity to repay family and village members their own sacrifices with the prestige and honor they generate as university students and members of a new elite" (Trueba and Zou 1994:131). Under China's system of Confucian values, education has always meant empowerment, not only for one's self, but for one's family as well. The practice of oppressed people gaining higher education expressly to serve their respective ethnic groups is a phenomenon that operates cross-culturally. (For example, see Huffman [1999] for a discussion of academic achievement motivation and American Indian education.)

This concludes the discussion of the two overarching, theoretical explanations of underachievement by minorities—the blocked opportunities explanation and the cultural differences explanation. The literature pertaining specifically to black, Hispanic and Indian students and academic achievement will be examined next.

Ethnic Identity and School Performance:
Research Pertaining to Specific Groups

Several multigroup ethnic identity models exist, such as the one developed by Jean Phinney (Phinney and Rotheram 1987; Phinney 1996). These look at the broad concept of an individual being part of a minority group. Most contemporary researchers, however, begin with the premise that not all ethnic groups or cultures are the same (Torres, Howard-Hamilton, and Cooper 2003). "Most would agree that Asian Americans, African Americans, Latino/Hispanic Americans, and American Indians each have a distinct cultural heritage that makes them different from each other" (Sue and Sue 1999:123). Thus, to better understand how students from these ethnic groups fare in school, it is important to look at research that pertains specifically to each of them.

What follows is a sample from a vast body of literature. The intent of this section is to give readers an overview of some of the key works on ethnic identity and academic achievement as they pertain to black, Hispanic and Indian students. This provides a context for understanding the model programs that serve underrepresented students in higher education to be discussed later in the book.

Broadly speaking, the literature selected for inclusion deals with the relationship of *ethnic identity* (generally treated as an independent variable) and *academic achievement* (generally treated as a dependent variable).

- *"Ethnic identity"* has been defined as "one's sense of belonging to an ethnic group and the part of one's thinking, perceptions, feelings, and behavior that is due to ethnic group membership" (Phinney and Rotheram 1987:13). Put simply, "ethnic identity" is a social-psychological construct that addresses the question "Who am I?" "Ethnicity" refers to group patterns, and "ethnic identity" refers to an individual's acquisition of these group patterns (Phinney and Rotheram 1987:13).
- *"Academic achievement"* has been defined as a measure of one's success within a formal educational system, as evaluated by some universally recognized hierarchy of common indicators (like grade point average, IQ, and math and reading achievement test scores). Sometimes academic achievement is judged by the volume of an individual's accomplishments, for example, by the number of academic awards received (Frisby 2001:541). Academic achievement is influenced by factors external and internal to the individual.

Hispanic students and academic achievement. Mexican Americans comprise most of all the Hispanic Americans living within the United States (Guzman 2001:2); therefore, most of the literature on Hispanic academic achievement focuses on them. Some articles about Chicano educational attainment are primarily methodological, exploring topics such as dialogical research (Padilla 1992) and biographical perspective (Galindo and Escamilla 1995).

Surprisingly, few articles point to cultural differences between home and school as a reason for Hispanic underachievement. A fair number of articles did, however, deal with Ogbu's notion of oppositional identities and how it relates to Hispanic students. A study of Puerto Rican high school students finds no evidence that the subjects underperformed in school because of a cultural opposition to "acting white" (Flores-Gonzalez 1999). Yet other research on Mexican-descent high school students supports Ogbu. For example, Maria Matute-Bianchi (1986:254) says that different students use different strategies to cope with the demands of schooling. "Students anticipate their future adult roles; develop a set of skills, behaviors, and instrumental orientations in response to those expectations and, in particular, respond to education in terms of its perceived role in their future." Finally, other research on Mexican American students shows no relationship whatsoever between ethnic identity and academic success (Okagaki, Frensch, and Dodson 1996).

Martha Bernal, Delia Saenz and George Knight (1991) argue for a "social identity approach" to making school work for Mexican American students. This social identity approach is a synthesis of the blocked opportunities theories and the cultural differences theories already discussed. The social identity approach suggests looking at the interaction of macro-ecological factors (such as poverty and discrimination) and micro-cultural factors (such as the difference between values taught at home and values taught at school) in order to explain minority student achievement.

Black students and academic achievement. Daphna Oyserman is another ethnicity scholar who grapples with the interrelationship of macro- and micro-level theory and research. The research program that she and numerous colleagues have pursued together over the past decade has focused primarily on African American identity and school performance, although this has recently branched out to include other ethnic groups as well.

Oyserman and her fellow researchers accept that macrosociological factors, like the low economic status of minorities (Ogbu 1992) and the pervasive presence of stereotypes (Steele 1997), do have debilitating effects on minority academic performance. The question remains, however, why individual members of the same ethnic group differ in their vulnerability to these threats and in their success in navigating the larger society (Oyserman et al. 2003:334). Oyserman's early work suggests that African American students who are successful manage to construct identities that help them achieve in school (Oyserman, Gant, and Ager 1995). The identity of such a student includes three components:

- connectedness to the black community,
- feeling that achievement is part of being black, and

• awareness of racism and other limitations.

Subsequent work by Oyserman and others (Oyserman, Harrison, and Bybee 2001) looks at the relationship of ethnic identity and academic efficacy. "Efficacy" means the power to influence one's environment and to control one's destiny. "Our project focused on academic efficacy because youth are more likely to invest effort in those endeavors they believe they are competent in and can succeed in," Oyserman, Harrison, and Bybee (2001:384) explain. Efficacy is a motivational force, a force that has a major impact on academic achievement. Individuals who believe they can "make it" are far more likely to actually "make it" than those who do not.

Oyserman found that a strong ethnic identity did indeed promote academic achievement, but the process worked differently for girls and boys. For girls, the "feeling that achievement is part of being black" component of ethnic identity promoted efficacy. For boys, the "connectedness to the black community" component of ethnic identity seemed to promote efficacy, but the relationship was not as strong. Nevertheless, the findings show that looking at ethnic identity and its effect on academic achievement as gender-specific holds promise for future research (Oyserman, Harrison, and Bybee 2001:384).

In a more recent research endeavor, Oyserman's team has looked at the "racial-ethnic self-schemas" of African American, Latino/a and Native American adolescents in the American Midwest and of Arab students in Israel (Oyserman et al. 2003).

Indian students and academic achievement. American Indians have been largely ignored in the literature on ethnic identity and academic achievement. A search of the past 20 years of refereed journals in sociology, psychology and education revealed 38 articles on African Americans, nine on Hispanic Americans and one on American Indians. (Databases searched were Sociological Abstracts, PsycINFO and ERIC. Eight of the articles found dealt with multiple ethnic groups.)

Similarly, ACE's *Annual Status Report* is considered *the* publication of record for documenting the educational attainment of minorities (Harvey 2003). Yet this report has a number of "recent trend" sections in which American Indians are not even mentioned, due to their relatively small number.

In the literature on American Indians that does exist, cultural difference has been identified most frequently as the factor that leads to underachievement. "Higher education reflects the dominant society's values and generally reinforces these or prevailing attitudes," Terry Huffman (1999:21) explains. "For students who are part of that cultural tradition, attending college simply requires moving deeper into their cultural milieu."

Curricula are standardized to teach students how to prosper in a white, middle-class society. The vast traditional knowledge of tribal people is largely ignored. The disinterest of American Indian students in learning material that is largely irrelevant to them has been cited frequently as a reason for dropping out (McDonald 1978). The experience of being Indian and attending a predominantly white university has been likened to being "refugees in an unknown country" (Steiner 1968:30).

John Reyhner (1992:37) agrees that micro-level cultural discontinuities between home and school are the primary reason for high Indian dropout rates. He cites seven specific reasons that Indians drop out— large schools, uncaring/untrained teachers, passive teaching methods, inappropriate curriculum, inappropriate testing/student retention in grade, tracked classes and lack of parent involvement.

In a recent study of ethnic identity and Indian higher education, Huffman (1999) has interviewed 69 Native American college students, some who drop out and others who persist through graduation. For Huffman's interviewees, the cultural differences they experience at college explain more of their academic problems than do any perceptions of blocked opportunities. "Assimilated students" (those who are most like non-Indian students) and "transcultured students" (those who can operate well in Indian and non-Indian cultures) are among the most successful in completing college. "Marginal students" are those who live on the margins of both Indian and non-Indian cultures, not completely breaking with past traditions and yet not fully accepted into the mainstream university. They are the third most successful group relative to college completion. "Estranged students," that is, those who feel that Native American culture is not celebrated or appreciated by the university, have the lowest graduation rates.

Other scholars say that too much emphasis has been placed on micro-level cultural discontinuities to explain Indian underachievement (Ledlow 1992). More attention needs to be paid to macrostructural determinants of school success. These scholars view the individual failure of Indian students as being caused largely by historical forces beyond their control. Indeed Ogbu (1978) himself classifies American Indians as a "castelike minority" whose opportunities for educational and economic success are routinely blocked.

Donna Deyhle has executed one of the few truly ethnographic studies of American Indian education to be completed recently. Deyhle (1992: 25) has spent seven years looking at Navajo and Ute students in reservation communities, with an eye toward "the role the school and structural barriers play in creating the problem" of dropping out. As Deyhle (1992:25) explains, "Structural factors restricting opportunities, in effect, 'fail' youth. The decision to leave school can then be seen, in part, as a rational response to irrelevant schooling, racism, restricted political, social and economic opportunities, and the desire to maintain a culturally distinct identity."

Summary and implications. This completes the brief review of literature dealing with Hispanic, black and Indian academic achievement. The theorists and researchers whose work was reviewed subscribe, in varying degrees, to either the cultural differences explanation or the blocked opportunities explanation of minority underachievement

There are those who view minority underachievement as resulting from primary cultural discontinuities, that is, cultural differences between the homes in which students are raised and the schools in which they will be educated. From this perspective, the problem of minority underachievement seems somewhat amenable to solution. Interventions focus on changing students' internal self-concepts, for example, by hosting campus celebrations of ethnicity or by hiring more culturally sensitive counselors (Huffman 1999).

Conversely, there are those who view minority underachievement as resulting from blocked opportunities. These scholars look to "secondary cultural differences," that is, differences that surface after students of color engage in the educational system of the dominant society, to explain minority underachievement. As articulated by Ogbu (1985:868), "children's school learning problems are ultimately caused by historical and structural forces beyond their control." In other words, the external social context blocks the educational and employment opportunities of such children, who are doomed to opt out of an educational system that to them appears meaningless. "It is likely that the degree of amenability to intervention of environmental factors will be a function of their proximity in the youths' social ecology," write Bernal, Saenz, and Knight (1991:149–150). "For example, classrooms, peers, teachers, school administrators, and textbooks may be more easily accessed for intervention than prevailing social attitudes embedded in public institutions."

Interventions That Increase Minority Access to College

How one views a problem determines, to a great extent, the proposed solution. Those who view minority underachievement from a cultural differences perspective favor interventions that focus on the individual, and those who view minority underachievement from a blocked opportunities perspective favor interventions that focus on the environment.

This book is about four highly effective interventions aimed at increasing minority access to college—Neighborhood Academic Initiative, 2+2+2, First Generation Student Success Program and Critical Moments. Although these programs have received national attention because of their effectiveness and uniqueness, they are certainly not the only programs of their kind. In the following sections, some other college preparation and retention efforts for minority students will be discussed.

College preparation. "Educational achievement between white students, on the one hand, and African American and Hispanic students, on the other, is large and persistent," write John Chubb and Tom Loveless (2002:1) of the Brookings Institution. "In the last decade it has gotten worse." Blacks and Hispanics are much less likely than whites to graduate from high school and to go on to college. Thus numerous programs have begun to remedy this situation. In their book titled *Bridging the Achievement Gap*, Chubb and Loveless describe some of these efforts: Project STAR (Student/Teacher Achievement Ratio) in Tennessee; the Student Achievement Guarantee in Education (SAGE) program in Wisconsin; the Knowledge Is Power Program (KIPP) in Los Angeles, Houston and New York; and Success for All, which operates in 48 states and 1,800 schools nationwide.

Sociologists of education have a particular interest in ethnic identity and its effect on academic achievement, so they have been in the forefront of efforts to help more students of color graduate from high school and prepare for college. Sociologist Hugh Mehan of the University of California, San Diego has studied an "untracking program" in a local high school. The program places Latino/a and African American students in college preparatory classes along with their high-achieving peers (Mehan et al. 1996). Participants in the program, called AVID (Advancement Via Individual Determination), did not display the "oppositional identities" that might be expected based on Ogbu's research. Rather, the AVID students accommodated to the norms of school without compromising their ethnic identity. Latino/a and African American students participating in AVID enrolled in four-year colleges at percentages well above the national average (Mehan, Hubbard, and Villanueva 1994).

"Culture, expressed as skills, habits, and styles, is the key to properly understanding ethnic and class differentials in cognitive achievement, and...these differences are the key to understanding earning inequality in American society," writes another sociologist, George Farkas (1996:5). Farkas's personal involvement with the school reform movement in Dallas led him to study the Reading One-One tutoring program. The program teaches reading to the lowest-performing elementary school children (primarily Hispanic and African American) in the system. Their reading gains were comparable to those of students enrolled in the most nationally successful one-on-one programs—gains achieved at less than one fourth the cost (Farkas 1996:175).

Both Farkas and Mehan are participants in the educational communities they study, not just outside observers. "While we conduct participant observation as do other ethnographers, we cannot leave the scene when we are finished," Mehan explains. "We live in the community we study, which means we are there the next day, supervising student teachers, consulting with principals, and contributing to school improvement efforts" (Mehan et al. 1996:22). The line between theory and praxis is thin to nonexistent for those concerned with ethnic identity, academic achievement and college access.

Daphna Oyserman of the University of Michigan, whose research was mentioned earlier, found that minority youth tend to do better in school if they have relatively complex beliefs about their ethnic identities. For the past four years, Oyserman and her associates have been conducting an after-school program for African American eighth graders in Detroit. The intent of the program is to make students' ethnic identities more complex through conscious interventions, and by so doing, foster academic success. One technique is helping students develop a "fight" rather than a "flight" response when they encounter prejudice and other obstacles to school success. Early results have been promising (Glenn 2003).

Carolyn Hodges and Olga Welch (2003:2) are two African American female professors at the University of Tennessee-Knoxville who describe themselves as "identified early as college material." "We found that our ability to succeed academically, even in the face of systemic racial and gender barriers, involved the development of a 'scholar identity,'" Hodges and Welch (2003:2) write. "The powerful nature of the scholar self in our own academic lives became the catalyst for the nine-year investigation of the relationship between academic achievement and identity construction presented in our book *Standing Outside on the Inside: Black Adolescents and the Construction of Academic Identity"* (Welch and Hodges 1997).

Hodges and Welch subsequently designed a summer school/ university enrichment program in order to look at the connection between precollege experiences and "scholar identity" development, primarily among African American students. This, in turn, led to Project EXCEL (Encouraging Excellence in Children Extends Learning). Project EXCEL is a college preparatory curriculum, offered in the center city school attended by the same college-bound students who participated in Hodges and Welch's initial summer school program. After three years of observing Project EXCEL, Hodges and Welch find that teacher/student interactions have a powerful effect on academic achievement. Hodges and Welch (2003:92) report, however, that "our data…did not provide definitive strategies for establishing a classroom in which students could construct definitions of scholar and scholarship positively correlated to achievement."

The idea that strengthening identity keeps students of color in school and moving toward higher education is a cornerstone of numerous precollege programs. William Morgan and Sandra Ezekiel (1995) look at a Saturday program offered at an African American heritage center. Morgan and Ezekiel find the program did little to develop ethnic identity, scholar identity or academic interest among the students who participated. Similarly Shawn Ginwright (2000) examines the introduction of an Afrocentric curriculum into an urban high school and finds no resulting improvement in academic performance. "I argue that the effort was ineffective because the project failed to consider the ways in which poverty influenced the identities of the students within the school," Ginwright (2000:87) says. Modest changes in K–12 schools, like Saturday programs and curriculum reform, seem to have little effect on the number of minority students attending college. Total school reform efforts—those that transmit a sense of ethnic identity, encourage academic achievement and provide guidance for pursuing higher education—seem much more effective.

"The formation of a personal identity in the context of schooling defines the opportunities for success and the relative power of the student to succeed," Trueba (2004:207) explains. "An ethnic, personal, and social identity is socially constructed in a given environment." Following are three examples of total school environments designed to strengthen ethnic identity and foster academic success.

- *Escuela Tlatelolco* is a small, private high school for Mexican students in Denver (McKissack 1999). Escuela Tlatelolco was founded in 1970 as an outgrowth of the Chicano Movement, which argued that public schools were not meeting the needs of the rapidly growing Hispanic student population. Although Escuela Tlatelolco follows a traditional academic curriculum, all classes are taught with an emphasis on Chicano identity, culture and history. By 1995 Escuela Tlatelolco had graduated more than 250 students, with an estimated 70 percent going on to college. Many of those graduates were initially classified as "at-risk" students. The school continues to follow Freire's philosophy that treats "action and experience as basic elements in the development of critical thinking" (McKissack 1999:26).
- *The Llano Grande Center for Research & Development* is a school- and community-based nonprofit organization located at Edcouch-Elsa High School in Elsa, Texas, 15 miles north of the Texas-Mexico border in the Rio Grande Valley (Guajardo and Guajardo 2002). The Center grew out of an ambitious oral history project, first undertaken by students in 1997 to explain the experience of Mexican people in the making of Texas. (This story was completely missing from the existing curriculum in a school where 99 percent of the student body was Mexican.)

  "Several hundred oral histories later, the project has been a source for the profound transformation of people, institutions, and even a community," explain Francisco Guajardo, the Center's executive director, and Miguel Guajardo, a board member (Guajardo and Guajardo 2002:286). Sixty low-income students from Edcouch-Elsa High School have been accepted at Ivy League schools (Guajardo and Guajardo 2002:287). Many of those students have returned to the Llano Grande Center to teach high school students, do community-based research and participate in development efforts (Guajardo and Guajardo 2002:288). "As we become stronger, we begin to dream and develop a 'pedagogy of hope,'" say Guajardo and Guajardo (2002:292), referring to the Freirean legacy and its continuing impact on the Llano Grande Center (Freire 1992).
- *South Dakota State University-Flandreau Indian School Success Academy* is an early and intensive college preparatory program for Native American high school students (Lee 2003). The program, which began in 2000, is a partnership between SDSU, the state's

land grant institution, and the nearby Flandreau Indian School (FIS), the country's oldest continually operating federal Indian boarding school. Success Academy's goals are to help more American Indian students prepare for and succeed in college—and to make SDSU into the kind of place where that can happen.

While much past effort has been spent trying to make Indian students fit into the existing white educational system, Success Academy takes a different tack. An important goal of the program is to make SDSU, a predominantly white university, into an institution that is appreciative of and responsive to Indian culture. Collaboration—between Indian educators and non-Indian educators, between university professors and K–12 teachers, between administrators and parents—is essential to the Success Academy program. The relationships that develop through Success Academy help FIS students prepare for college, a step most consider impossible before starting the program. Many FIS students come from backgrounds where they experience high levels of poverty, persistent chemical dependency and numerous other problems.

Success Academy students (virtually all the students attending FIS) spend 15 full days at SDSU during their freshman, sophomore and junior years of high school. Success Academy Scholars, as the students are called, attend academic workshops, evening meals and campus events, presented by 250 SDSU faculty members and an equal number of SDSU students, both Indian and non-Indian. As seniors, the Success Academy students enroll in regular university classes, which bring them to the SDSU campus once every week during their last year of high school. The promotion of ethnic identity throughout all the programming is an essential part of the Success Academy philosophy. This is in keeping with Freire's notion of "conscientization," the process through which oppressed people realize that their cultural values are legitimate and worth maintaining (Freire 2002). In its first five years, Success Academy increased college attendance among FIS participants by 500 percent.

College retention. Increasing the number of minority students who receive bachelor's degrees requires attention to four critical junctures: academic preparation for college, graduation from high school, enrollment in college and persistence in college (Swail 2003:11). The first two junctures have been discussed in the previous section; the last two junctures will be discussed in this section.

While minority participation in higher education has increased significantly, students of color still are not staying in school and graduating with the same success as white students. African American and Hispanic students are about half as likely as their white peers to complete four years of college. The mood of the country, however, now seems to be one of cost-cutting at the expense of educational access, according to a recent study by the American Association of State Colleges and Universities (AASCU) (1997:2–3). "Many policymakers seem to be able to overlook the need to help any person who is denied or excluded opportunities—and thus benefits—because he is disadvantaged," the AASCU (1997:3) maintains. Increasingly, education is viewed as a private benefit rather than a benefit to society as a whole (AASCU 1997:3).

Due to the severity of the problem, much has been written about retention efforts for minority students. Only a brief overview of this material will be presented here. This is to give context to the forthcoming discussion of the four model programs that are the focus of this book and that involve minority student retention.

Campus climate is a major theme running throughout the literature on minority student retention. "From the minority student's perspective, the climate of the campus is made up of all the subtle and not so subtle ways in which attitudes are expressed," write Barbara Astone and Elsa Nunez-Wormack (1990:63). Astone and Nunez-Wormack (1990:64–68) identify four aspects of campus climate that affect the retention of students of color—curriculum, critical mass, role models and programs enhancing diversity. Each of these will be discussed in some detail below.

• *Curriculum:* Students need to see their culture reflected in what is taught in the classroom and what is studied (and valued) by faculty members.

One example of successful curricular reform is Indiana University's Project TEAM (Transformative Educational Achievement Model). Project TEAM was begun in 1996 to increase the number of students of color who enter the teacher education program, complete their baccalaureate degrees and join the teaching profession (Bennett 2002). The centerpiece of the program is an honors seminar based on collaborative learning and multicultural studies. As described by the Project TEAM director, Christine Bennett (2002):

The honors seminar…provides an academic setting where minority students can study exclusively with student peers of color, in addition to their other classes where few if any students of color are present....Students have an opportunity to share personal experiences dealing with racism and prejudice (on and off campus); gain awareness of other cultures; and discover the multiple differences as well as similarities within a single minority group of students, in this case African Americans and Latinos. (P. 27)

• *Critical mass:* The issue of critical mass can best be explained by the response of one student of color, when asked why she chose to attend a particular college: "'There are other minorities there, so I don't have to feel like a Martian.'...No matter how outstanding the academic institution, ethnic minority students can feel alienated if their ethnic representation on campus is small" (Loo and Rolison 1986:69, 72).

An example of promising practice in increasing critical mass is the University of Wisconsin's Design for Diversity, a ten-year systemwide plan to increase the number of new black, Hispanic and Indian students by 100 percent. The Design for Diversity began in 1988 to create "a multicultural teaching and learning environment, one that effectively prepares all students to live and work in a pluralistic society. The plan targets institutional racism and seeks to eradicate its negative impact on the system's campuses" (Hurtado et al. 1999:91). During its first five years, Design for Diversity achieved 80 percent of its goals for student enrollment each year, increasing the number of undergraduate students of color from 1,270 to 2,540.

• *Role models:* The presence of successful people of color has a positive, motivating effect on minority college students (Astone and Nunez-Wormack 1990:67).

One such effort to provide positive role models for students of color is the Black Man's Think Tank, a mentoring program for African American men at the University of Cincinnati (LaVant, Anderson, and Tiggs 1997:46). The Think Tank is a forum for black male academicians to discuss issues confronting black male college students. The Think Tank matches black male students with black male professionals. Setting priorities, balancing male-female relationships, learning to sacrifice and giving back to the black community are all topics addressed during discussions between the mentors and the mentees.

• *Programs enhancing diversity:* Ethnic studies programs, academic support programs and social programs all play an important part in the retention of students of color. Social programs include multicultural events on campus and organizations for minority students.

A new trend to surface in recent years is SIRPs—student-initiated retention projects (Rhoads, Buenavista, and Maldonado 2004). SIRPs involve ethnic student organizations like the Movimiento Estudiantil Chicano de Aztlan and the Black Student Union banding together to serve students of color on their respective campuses. This has occurred in response to the perception that universities are limited in their ability to serve the needs of diverse student communities.

There is definitely a Freirean quality to SIRPs. "Paulo Freire...argued that learning must become an act of self-empowerment in order to have real significance for an individual," writes Rhoads et al. (2004:12), who together with his colleagues spent three years studying SIRPs. "Student-of-color organizers see the success of their racial and ethnic communities as tied to their own efforts to support one another and to challenge university structures that do not adequately meet the needs of their communities."

The SIRPs studied by Rhoads and his colleagues have three elements in common. First, SIRPs develop cultural and social capital, that is, important forms of knowledge needed for success in college and professional life. Second, SIRPs enhance community consciousness and develop commitments to particular ethnic communities and to the broader community of color. Third, SIRPs promote social praxis by challenging institutional norms that limit the success of students of color (Rhoads et al. 2004:14–16).

The newest literature addressing minority student retention focuses on the transformative power of education for both students of color and the universities they attend. Discussing this literature brings us full circle to where Chapter One began. Universities are encouraged to abandon the old "deficit model" once used in working with minority students and instead adopt an "assets-based" approach. In their new book, *Transforming the First Year of College for Students of Color*, Laura Rendon, Mildred Garcia and Dawn Person (2004) note that:

> Many students of color can be considered survivors. They have survived oppressive experiences such as poverty, racism, discrimination, prejudice, stereotyping, marginalization, and exploitation. They have endured schools that have offered them the least experienced teachers, the worst learning conditions, and the lowest expectations...However, educators should note that many students of color, who have managed to enroll in college as first-year students, bring some important assets such as mastering different languages, maneuvering multiple realities (i.e., the world of work, ghetto, barrio, reservation, gang culture, family, and schooling) and negotiating social, political, and economic hardships. (Pp. 4–5)

Another recent volume, *How Minority Students Experience College*, reminds student affairs professionals (the book's primary audience), that "as educators, we should ensure that every voice is heard in order to bring about a greater understanding of students' experiences, beliefs, and values" (Watson, Terrell, and Wright 2002:106).

In short, working with students of color to make sure they succeed in school involves more than just supplying those students with the necessary social and cultural capital to persist through graduation. Rather, this work involves challenging the entire culture of higher education. The culture of higher education is a culture that does not recognize the legitimacy of nonstandard English dialects or the value of speaking multiple languages (Terrell and Wright 1988:26). It is a culture that allows acts of intolerance on campus in the name of freedom of speech. And it is a culture where dissension about multicultural education runs rampant, where whites openly argue that students of color receive special privileges that constitute reverse discrimination.

Those working most fervently today for the retention of more students of color on campus argue that significant change will occur only by "improving the climate for racial/ethnic diversity in higher education" (Hurtado et al. 1999). This view meshes perfectly with that of the chapter authors, whose work constitutes the remainder of this book.

The Personal

The collection of information for a book usually has a logic that emerges from the personal story of the author. A book is better understood when the readers know something about the writer.

In 1991, my husband, Richard W. Lee, and I were chosen by our university, South Dakota State, to spend a semester as exchange professors at our sister school, Yunnan Normal (Teachers) University. Yunnan Province, in the far southwest of the People's Republic of China (PRC), is home to 25 of the PRC's 55 officially recognized "minority nationality" groups. Most of these groups are severely disadvantaged, having experienced significant discrimination throughout much of China's history.

In China, the obstacles to acquiring a good education are considerable. Only about two percent of all college-age youth can enroll in universities, so the odds against being admitted are great even for the average Han majority Chinese. For minority nationality students, the odds against being accepted into college and then attaining a degree are truly staggering.

As exchange professors in China, we were privileged to teach a considerable number of ethnic minority students who had beat the odds and won college admittance. These students managed to function effectively in a university culture distinctly different from the ones in which they had been raised. In many cases, these students learned and were tested in a language (Mandarin Chinese) different from their native ones. As the minority nationality students in our classes got to know us better, they told us their life stories. In many cases, these students had overcome almost insurmountable obstacles in order to achieve their educational and professional goals.

How were these successful minority students in China able to do that? What role did a strong ethnic identity play, in the educational achievement of the students themselves, and also ultimately in the empowerment of their minority groups? Finding the answers to these questions drew me back to China, six years after that initial exchange experience. During the Summer of 1997, I returned to Yunnan Province, this time in the role of a doctoral student in Rural Sociology at SDSU. I collected data, first for my dissertation and later for a book titled *Ethnicity, Education and Empowerment: How Minority Students in Southwest China Construct Identities* (Lee 2001).

The emphasis in *Ethnicity, Education and Empowerment* was on *micro*-sociological theorizing. At that time I was interested in learning how individual ethnic minority students—interacting with their relatives, school teachers and nationality groups—socially constructed identities that allowed them to succeed in school. The focus was on *agency*, that is, how minority students and their reference groups created "achievement-oriented selves" (Lee 2001:64), selves that allowed these students to succeed in an educational system where many other ethnic students failed. (Work by Oyserman on "achievement-related possible selves" and black student achievement, described in detail earlier in this chapter, provided major insights for the China study.) An agency perspective suggests the freedom of individuals to create changes in society from the bottom up, rather than from the top down.

The most significant finding to grow out of the China project was this: *A strong ethnic identity can empower an individual to succeed academically.* At the end of the China book, I attempted to explain how this finding was relevant to American educators struggling with questions of minority underachievement. A final section of *Ethnicity, Education and Empowerment* was on selective approaches to educational reform in the United States. I described four innovative programs in the United States that put into practice some of the same techniques used by

Chinese educators to help minority students succeed in school. These four innovative programs were Neighborhood Academic Initiative, 2+2+2, First Generation Student Success Program and Critical Moments. Even as I wrote the final pages of that volume, briefly touching on these four programs, I knew I wanted to learn more about them.

Shortly after the completion of *Ethnicity, Education and Empowerment*, in the Spring of 2001, an opportunity arose to merge theory with praxis in my professional life, then as a clinical sociologist at South Dakota State University. Together with two colleagues from the nearby Flandreau Indian School, Sandra Koester and Susan Mendelsohn, I helped launch the SDSU-FIS Success Academy project, an early and intensive college preparatory program for American Indian students. (This coincided with the adoption by FIS of a comprehensive school reform plan, called Talent Development High School, created by the Johns Hopkins University Center for the Social Organization of Schools.)

The goals of SDSU-FIS Success Academy, described earlier in this chapter, are to help more American Indian students prepare for and succeed in college—and to make SDSU into the kind of place where that can happen. Put another way, Success Academy attempts:

- to use and enhance the "cultural wealth" (Yosso 2005) Indian students bring to school with them in order to help them earn college degrees; and
- to work toward fundamental systemic change at the state's largest—and predominantly white—university.

In the process of creating the SDSU-FIS Success Academy, we searched nationwide for model programs that were highly effective in preparing students from underrepresented groups for college and in supporting these students through baccalaureate degree completion. Consequently, in the Fall of 2002, SDSU hosted a conference called "Ethnicity Matters—Rethinking How Black, Hispanic and Indian Students Prepare for and Succeed in College," featuring speakers from the NAI, 2+2+2, the FGSSP and Critical Moments.

The keynote speaker for the conference was Dr. Enrique (Henry) T. Trueba. Henry was then the Ruben E. Hinojosa Regents Professor Emeritus in the College of Education at the University of Texas, Austin. He was also the author of 24 books focused on ethnicity, education and empowerment of minorities. Most importantly, at least for me, Henry was my long-time mentor, teacher and friend. In fact, the study he did (with Yali Zou) of Miao nationality students in Beijing and Guizhou in

1992 (Trueba and Zou 1994) in large part inspired my own research on minority nationality students in Yunnan Province in 1997 (Lee 2001).

Although we were geographically separated by half a continent, Henry's influence on my work and life has been, and continues to be, enormous. Henry passed on to the next life, after a long battle with cancer, in July 2004. During the last year of his life, it was a rare day that an e-mail did not go back and forth, linking the two of us, one in South Dakota and the other in South Texas.

Henry had worked with Paulo Friere, George Spindler, Louise Spindler and countless other major scholars of the twentieth century. With them, he developed key ideas on critical pedagogy, cultural therapy and empowerment, ideas that influenced his own life's work and later the life's work of hundreds of Ph.D. students and colleagues, I among them.

Because of Henry, I regularly reflect on the educational system that I have been part of for the past 45 years—as a student, as a teacher, as a researcher and as an administrator. And I now view that system in a fundamentally different way. Most of the schools I attended (and most of the schools that employed me) seemed to me at the time to be institutions genuinely committed to democratic ends. In actuality, I believe they achieved quite the opposite. Upon reflection, these schools clearly disempowered some students, while preparing others for success (Trueba and Zou 1994:12–13).

I wonder now if I have been part of the problem. Did I participate in replicating educational structures that benefited me, at the expense of others? As I ask myself these questions, I also invite those around me—students, colleagues, scholars and most particularly the readers of this book—to join me in this reflection.

As critical theorists, we must continually question how race, class and gender affect the positions we occupy in the academic hierarchy. How will we use whatever power and privilege we accrue to work toward an educational system that ensures greater equity?

My intention is to pursue these topics in the years ahead. The publication of *Ethnicity Matters* is a logical next step. In this book the emphasis is on *macro*-sociological theorizing. Led by the chapter authors, we will consider how the culture, the norms and the values of schooling all must change in order to empower students of color to succeed academically. Our focus will be on the *structure* of schooling itself, viewed as a determinant of individual student achievement.

"One of the major criticisms of critical theory is that individuals cannot often envision what abstract ideas look like when they are employed," Tierney (2000:214) writes. His point is well taken. Sharing our stories is crucial. In this way we teach each other what is possible.

College preparation and retention programs that stress minority student assimilation into mainstream academic culture have been well documented in the existing literature. Still, American universities remain predominantly white institutions, excluding all but a few students of color and not reflecting the ethnic diversity of the United States. Continuing to document failure only demonstrates the obvious.

This book takes a different tack, one that is well captured by the words of the late sociologist Robert Merton (1968:490): "More is learned from the single success than from the multiple failures. A single success proves it can be done. Thereafter, it is necessary only to learn what made it work."

The remainder of this volume will focus on four successful attempts to reform minority education in the United States. The four programs discussed in the following chapters involve black, Hispanic and Indian students, individuals from those ethnic groups that face the most serious problems of underrepresentation in American higher education. As authors, we will argue that a strong ethnic identity can empower a student of color to succeed academically. Programs that affirm and honor individual identities *do* work. Ethnicity *does* matter. The programs described in the following chapters—Neighborhood Academic Initiative, 2+2+2, First Generation Student Success Program and Critical Moments—are all substantially increasing the number of minority individuals with college degrees.

References

Akom, A. A. 2003. "Reexamining Resistance as Oppositional Behavior: The Nation of Islam and the Creation of a Black Achievement Ideology." *Sociology of Education* 76:305–325.

American Association of State Colleges and Universities. 1997. *Policies and Practice: Focus on Higher Education Retention*. Washington, D.C.: American Association of State Colleges and Universities.

American Council on Education. 2004. *Reflections on 20 Years of Minorities in Higher Education and the ACE Annual Status Report*. Washington, D.C.: American Council on Education.

Arroyo, Carmen G. and Edward Zigler. 1995. "Racial Identity, Academic Achievement, and the Psychological Well-Being of Economically Disadvantaged Adolescents." *Journal of Personality and Social Psychology* 69:903–914.

Astone, Barbara and Elsa Nunez-Wormack. 1990. *Pursuing Diversity: Recruiting College Minority Students*. Washington, D.C.: School of Education and Human Development, George Washington University.

Bennett, Christine I. 2002. "Enhancing Ethnic Diversity at a Big Ten University Through Project TEAM: A Case Study in Teacher Education." *Educational Researcher* 31(2):21–29.

Bergin, David A. and Helen C. Cooks. 2002. "High School Students of Color Talk About Accusations of 'Acting White.'" *The Urban Review* 34:113–134.

Bernal, Martha E., Delia S. Saenz, and George P. Knight. 1991. "Ethnic Identity and Adaptation of Mexican American Youths in School Settings." *Hispanic Journal of Behavioral Sciences* 13:135–154.

Bourdieu, Pierre. 1977. "Cultural Reproduction and Social Reproduction." Pp. 487–511 in *Power and Ideology in Education*, edited by J. Karabel and A. H. Halsey. New York: Oxford University Press.

Chapell, Mark S. and Willis F. Overton. 2002. "Development of Logical Reasoning and the School Performance of African American Adolescents in Relation to Socioeconomic Status, Ethnic Identity, and Self-Esteem." *Journal of Black Psychology* 28:295–317.

Chubb, John and Tom Loveless, eds. 2002. *Bridging the Achievement Gap*. Washington, D.C.: Brookings Institution Press.

Datnow, Amanda and Robert Cooper. 1997. "Peer Networks of African American Students in Independent Schools: Affirming Academic Success and Racial Identity." *The Journal of Negro Education* 66:56–72.

Deyhle, Donna. 1992. "Constructing Failure and Maintaining Cultural Identity: Navajo and Ute School Leavers." *Journal of American Indian Education* 31(1):24–47.

Durkheim, Emile. 1951. *Suicide*. New York: The Free Press.

Farkas, George. 1996. *Human Capital or Cultural Capital?: Ethnicity and Poverty Groups in an Urban School*. New York: Aldine de Gruyter.

Flores-Gonzalez, Nilda. 1999. "Puerto Rican High Achievers: An Example of Ethnic and Academic Identity Compatibility." *Anthropology & Education Quarterly* 30:343–362.

Ford, Donna Y., J. John Harris III, Karen S. Webb, and Deneese L. Jones. 1994. "Rejection or Confirmation of Racial identity: A Dilemma for High-Achieving Blacks?" *The Journal of Educational Thought* 28:7–33.

Fordham, Signithia. 1988. "Racelessness as a Factor in Black Students' School Success: Pragmatic Strategy or Pyrrhic Victory." *Harvard Educational Review* 58:54–84.

———. 1996. *Blacked Out: Dilemmas of Race, Identity, and Success at Capital High*. Chicago: The University of Chicago Press.

Fordham, Signithia and John U. Ogbu. 1986. "Black Students' School Success: Coping with the 'Burden of Acting White.'" *The Urban Review* 18:176–206.

Foucault, Michel. 1983. "Afterword." Pp. 208–264 in *Michel Foucault: Beyond Structuralism and Hermeneutics*, by H. L. Dreyfus and P. Rabinow. Chicago: The University of Chicago Press.

Freire, Paulo. 1992. *Pedagogy of Hope*. New York: Continuum.

———. 2002. *Pedagogy of the Oppressed*. (30th Anniversary Ed.). New York: Continuum.

Frisby, Craig L. 2001. "Academic Achievement." Pp. 541–568 in *Handbook of Multicultural Assessment: Clinical, Psychological, and Educational Applications*, edited by L. A. Suzuki, J. G. Ponterotto, and P. J. Meller. San Francisco: Jossey-Bass Publishers.

Galindo, Rene and Kathy Escamilla. 1995. "A Biographical Perspective on Chicano Educational Success." *The Urban Review* 27:1–29.

Ginwright, Shawn A. 2000. "Identity for Sale: The Limits of Racial Reform in Urban Schools." *The Urban Review* 32:87–104.

Glenn, David. 2003, June 2. "Minority Students With Complex Beliefs About Ethnic Identity Are Found to Do Better in School." *The Chronicle of Higher Education*. Retrieved July 17, 2003, from http://chronicle.com/daily/2003/06/2003060201n.htm

Guajardo, Miguel A. and Francisco J. Guajardo. 2002. "Critical Ethnography and Community Change." Pp. 281–304 in *Ethnography* and Schools: Qualitative Approaches to the Study of Education, edited by Y. Zou and H. T. Trueba. Lanham, Md.: Rowman & Littlefield Publishers.

Guzman, Betsy. 2001. "The Hispanic Population: Census 2000 Brief." *United States Census 2000* May:1-8.

Hall, C. Jean Mosley. 1998. "The Association Between Racelessness and Achievement Among African American Deaf Adolescents." *American Annals of the Deaf* 143:55–64.

Harvey, William B. 2003. *20ᵗʰ Anniversary Minorities in Higher Education Annual Status Report*. Washington, D.C.: American Council on Education.

Hodges, Carolyn R. and Olga M. Welch. 2003. *Making Schools Work: Negotiating Educational Meaning and Transforming the Margins*. New York: Peter Lang.

Horvat, Erin McNamara and Kristine S. Lewis. 2003. "Reassessing the 'Burden of Acting White': The Importance of Peer Groups in Managing Academic Success." *Sociology of Education* 76:265–280.

Huffman, Terry E. 1999. *Cultural Masks: Ethnic Identity and American Indian Higher Education*. Buckhannon, W.Va.: Stone Creek Press.

Hurtado, Sylvia, Jeffrey Milem, Alma Clayton-Pedersen, and Walter Allen. 1999. *Enacting Diverse Learning Environments: Improving the Climate for Racial/Ethnic Diversity in Higher Education*. Washington, D.C.: School of Education and Human Development, George Washington University.

Iber, George Leland. 1992. "Academic Performance, Acculturation and Ethnic Identity Traits of First and Second Generation Mexican-American High School Students in a Rural Iowa Town." Ph.D. dissertation, College of Education, University of Iowa, Iowa City, Iowa.

Kanpol, Barry. 1994. *Critical Pedagogy: An Introduction*. Westport, Conn.: Bergin & Garvey.

Kao, Grace, Marta Tienda, and Barbara Schneider. 1996. "Racial and Ethnic Variation in Academic Performance." *Research in Sociology of Education and Socialization* 11:263–297.

LaVant, Bruce D., John L. Anderson, and Joseph W. Tiggs. 1997. "Retaining African American Men Through Mentoring Initiatives." Pp. 43–53 in *Helping African American Men Succeed in College*, edited by M. J. Cuyjet. San Francisco: Jossey-Bass Publishers.

Ledlow, Susan. 1992. "Is Cultural Discontinuity an Adequate Explanation for Dropping Out?" *Journal of American Indian Education* 31(3):21–36.

Lee, MaryJo Benton. 2001. *Ethnicity, Education and Empowerment: How Minority Students in Southwest China Construct Identities.* Burlington, Vt.: Ashgate.

———. 2003. "A College Preparatory Program for Native American Students: SDSU-Flandreau Indian School Success Academy." Presented at the annual meeting of the American Sociological Association, August 18, Atlanta, Ga.

Loo, Chalsa M. and Garry Rolison. 1986. "Alienation of Ethnic Minority Students at a Predominantly White University." *Journal of Higher Education* 57:58–77.

Matute-Bianchi, Maria Eugenia. 1986. "Ethnic Identities and Patterns of School Success and Failure among Mexican-Descent and Japanese-American Students in a California High School: An Ethnographic Analysis." *American Journal of Education* 95:233–255.

McDonald, Arthur. 1978. "Why Do Indian Students Drop Out of College?" Pp. 73–85 in *The Schooling of Native America*, edited by T. Thompson. Washington, D.C.: American Association of Colleges for Teacher Education.

McKissack, Elena Aragon de. 1999. *Chicano Educational Achievement: Comparing Escuela Tlatelolco, a Chicanocentric School, and a Public High School.* New York: Taylor & Francis.

Mehan, Hugh, Irene Villanueva, Lea Hubbard, and Angela Lintz. 1996. *Constructing School Success: The Consequences of Untracking Low-Achieving Students.* New York: Cambridge University Press.

Mehan, Hugh, Lea Hubbard, and Irene Villanueva. 1994. "Forming Academic Identities: Accommodation without Assimilation among Involuntary Minorities." *Anthropology & Education Quarterly* 25:91–117.

Merton, Robert K. 1968. *Social Theory and Social Structure.* New York: The Free Press.

Morgan, William and Sandra Ezekiel. 1995. "Supplementary Education for African American Children at Risk." *Applied Behavioral Science Review* 3:147–163.

Ogbu, John U. 1978. *Minority Education and Caste.* New York: Academic Press.

———. 1985. "Research Currents: Cultural-Ecological Influences on Minority School Learning." *Language Arts* 62:860–869.

———. 1992. "Understanding Cultural Diversity and Learning." *Educational Researcher* 21(8):5–24.

Okagaki, Lynn, Peter A. Frensch, and Nedra Evette Dodson. 1996. "Mexican American Children's Perceptions of Self and School

Achievement." *Hispanic Journal of Behavioral Sciences* 18:469–484.

Oyserman, Daphna, Kathy Harrison, and Deborah Bybee. 2001. "Can Racial Identity Be Promotive of Academic Efficacy?" *International Journal of Behavioral Development* 25:379–385.

Oyserman, Daphna, Larry Gant, and Joel Ager. 1995. "A Socially Contextualized Model of African American Identity: Possible Selves and School Persistence." *Journal of Personality and Social Psychology* 69:1216–1232.

Oyserman, Daphna, Markus Kemmelmeier, Stephanie Fryberg, Hezi Brosh, and Tamera Hart-Johnson. 2003. "Racial-Ethnic Self-Schemas." *Social Psychology Quarterly* 66:333–347.

Padilla, Raymond V. 1992. "Using Dialogical Research Methods to Study Chicano College Students." *The Urban Review* 24:175–183.

Phinney, Jean S. 1996. "Understanding Ethnic Diversity: The Role of Ethnic Identity." *American Behavioral Scientist* 40:143–152.

Phinney, Jean S. and Mary Jane Rotheram, eds. 1987. *Children's Ethnic Socialization: Pluralism and Development.* Newbury Park, Calif.: SAGE Publications.

Rendon, Laura I., Mildred Garcia, and Dawn Person, eds. 2004. *Transforming the First Year of College for Students of Color.* Columbia, S.C.: The National Resource Center for the First-Year Experience & Students in Transition.

Rendon, Laura I., Romero E. Jalomo, and Amaury Nora. 2000. "Theoretical Considerations in the Study of Minority Student Retention in Higher Education." Pp. 127–156 in *Reworking the Student Departure Puzzle,* edited by J. M. Braxton. Nashville: Vanderbilt University Press.

Reyhner, Jon. 1992. "American Indians Out of School: A Review of School-Based Causes and Solutions." *Journal of American Indian Education* 31(3):37–56.

Rhoads, Robert A., Tracy Lachica Buenavista, and David E. Z. Maldonado. 2004. "Students of Color Helping Others Stay in College: A Grassroots Effort." *About Campus* 9(3):10–17.

Steele, Claude M. 1997. "A Threat in the Air: How Stereotypes Shape Intellectual Identity and Performance." *American Psychologist* 52:613–629.

Steiner, Stan. 1968. *The New Indians.* New York: Harper & Row Publishers.

Sue, Derald Wing and David Sue. 1999. *Counseling the Culturally Different: Theory and Practice.* New York: John Wiley & Sons.

Swail, Watson Scott. 2003. *Retaining Minority Students in Higher Education: A Framework for Success.* San Francisco: Wiley Periodicals.

Taylor, Donald M. 1997. "The Quest for Collective Identity: The Plight of Disadvantaged Ethnic Minorities." *Canadian Psychology* 38:174–190.

Taylor, Ronald D., Robin Casten, Susanne M. Flickinger, Debra Roberts, and Cecil D. Fulmore. 1994. "Explaining the School Performance of African-American Adolescents." *Journal of Research on Adolescence* 4:21–44.

Terrell, Melvin C. and Doris J. Wright, eds. 1988. *From Survival to Success: Promoting Minority Student Retention.* Washington, D.C.: National Association of Student Personnel Administration.

Tierney, William G. 1993. *Building Communities of Difference: Higher Education in the Twenty-First Century.* Toronto, Ontario: OISE Press.

———. 2000. "Power, Identity and the Dilemma of College Student Departure." Pp. 213–234 in *Rethinking the Student Departure Puzzle,* edited by J. M. Braxton. Nashville: Vanderbilt University Press.

Tinto, Vincent. 1975. "Dropout from Higher Education: A Theoretical Synthesis of Recent Research." *Review of Educational Research* 45:89–125.

———. 1993. *Leaving College: Rethinking the Causes and Cures of Student Attrition.* Chicago: The University of Chicago Press.

Torres, Vasti, Mary F. Howard-Hamilton, and Diane L. Cooper. 2003. *Identity Development of Diverse Populations: Implications for Teaching and Administration in Higher Education.* San Francisco: Jossey-Bass Publishers.

Trueba, Enrique (Henry) T. 2004. *The New Americans: Immigrants and Transnationals at Work.* Lanham, Md.: Rowman & Littlefield Publishers.

Trueba, Henry T. 1988. "Culturally Based Explanations of Minority Students' Academic Achievement." *Anthropology & Education Quarterly* 19:270–287.

Trueba, Henry T. and Yali Zou. 1994. *Power in Education: The Case of Miao University Students and its Significance for American Culture.* Washington, D.C.: The Falmer Press.

Trueba, Henry T., Lila Jacobs, and Elizabeth Kirton. 1990. *Cultural Conflict and Adaptation: The Case of Hmong Children in American Society.* New York: The Falmer Press.

Watson, Lemuel, Melvin C. Terrell, and Doris J. Wright. 2002. *How Minority Students Experience College.* Bolton, Mass.: Anker Publishing Company.

Welch, Olga M. and Carolyn Hodges. 1997. *Standing Outside on the Inside: Black Adolescents and the Construction of Academic Identity.* Albany: State University of New York Press.

Yosso, Tara J. 2005. "Whose Culture Has Capital? A Critical Race Theory Discussion of Community Cultural Wealth." *Race Ethnicity and Education* 8:69–91.

2
Neighborhood Academic Initiative: Connecting Culture and College Preparation

Julia E. Colyar

"Purpose: The Neighborhood Academic Initiative (NAI) provides multiple educational opportunities for students and parents to gain an understanding of themselves and to obtain the skills needed to achieve college success."
—From the Neighborhood Academic Initiative Web Site

When Tiffanie Morgan and her family moved from San Francisco to Los Angeles, she was 11 years old. The family settled in a neighborhood south of downtown, commonly referred to as "South Central LA," a predominantly African American community. Before they had unpacked their boxes, Tiffanie's father set out to find a school for his daughters. "He wanted us to go to college; he just went around and talked to people," Tiffanie said. At Foshay Learning Center, a school serving students from kindergarten through twelfth grade, Mr. Morgan found the Neighborhood Academic Initiative (NAI). Tiffanie arrived at Foshay the following Monday with a blue backpack and started sixth grade. Seven years later, she enrolled as a freshman at the University of Southern California (USC). (All names in the chapter are pseudonyms.)

The Neighborhood Academic Initiative

The NAI was developed in 1990 as a partnership between USC, the Los Angeles Unified School District and two local high schools. Each year NAI admits a small cohort of seventh grade students (25 to 40 students) into the Pre-College Academy, which provides support and academic enrichment through middle and high school, and ultimately, into college. Students in the program come from neighborhoods with historically low representation in postsecondary institutions; the majority of the students are African American or Latino/a, and many come from immigrant families. Students chosen to participate are "B" or "C" students; they do not need to be "Straight A" students or carry the expectation that they will go to an elite college. The rationale for this selection process is simple: "Straight A" students typically gain the attention of school teachers and officials, while "B" and "C" students are sometimes overlooked. These students, program staff believe, can be supported and encouraged to love learning. Program directors look for promise and willingness to work; students are chosen based on their stated willingness to learn and a parent or guardian's willingness to provide support. In most cases, students fit within the characteristics of "at risk": first generation college students, from low-income communities and from groups historically underrepresented in higher education (Horn and Chen 1998). Some of the students read at levels below their current grade.

During the first two hours of each school day, NAI students attend accelerated classes in English and mathematics at the USC campus. Instructors are chosen, hired and trained by NAI personnel, but come from local high schools. Following morning classes, buses take the students the short distances to their home schools where they complete the school day. Students are also required to attend the "Saturday Enrichment Academy" each week, also on the USC campus, where they take classes in areas such as test preparation, time management, critical thinking and computer skills. During the summer, students take extra enrichment courses.

Throughout the years of the program, students are always referred to as "Scholars," a label intended to help students *see* themselves as successful students and future college-goers. This distinction is also part of the program's development of a college-going culture among program participants. From the start of the program in seventh grade, students are counted as individuals who have the potential and motivation to succeed in their goal to complete an undergraduate degree.

One of the most important principles of the NAI program is the active inclusion of family in the educational process. Parents or guardians must agree to encourage their children to study after school and to notify NAI staff when they are having troubles at home. While students attend Saturday sessions, parents attend family-oriented sessions approximately once per month. Workshops are delivered in Spanish and English and pertain to a variety of issues, including parenting strategies and creating a study environment in the home. Preparing program materials in Spanish is an important detail that invites parents into the educational process. Oftentimes, families are excluded from their children's academic experiences simply because of language barriers. Recognizing languages other than English subtly validates the parents' importance in the program. Parents are also required to attend all NAI-sponsored activities, and they must volunteer to assist NAI staff in at least one program per year. Every parent or guardian is also a member of one of the family committees.

NAI's commitment to family engagement is one of the program features aimed at affirming students' local identities. As William Tierney and Alexander Jun (2001) point out, the program's name is purposive; the "neighborhood" is an integral aspect of program success. Many college preparation programs suggest that families and communities somehow hold students back or are detrimental to young people's progress into higher education. Many programs remove youth from their neighborhoods and place them in preparatory or private schools, far from urban settings. NAI, however, "assumes that academic success is tied to the student's ability to relate to his or her local neighborhood contexts" (Tierney and Jun 2001:214). Parents, guardians, extended family and community members are essential components of the learning process, particularly as students learn about themselves. In order to reinforce the positive aspects of student contexts, teachers and counselors are often from the local communities themselves and are frequently from underrepresented groups. Their positions afford them understandings of the particular challenges students in the community face. Community leaders and mentors are also invited to meet with students and parents at Saturday programs. NAI students are encouraged to act as mentors for younger siblings and neighbors. The program works in a systematic way to affirm the students' conceptions of themselves and to celebrate their cultures and communities.

Equally important to utilizing local identities is the program's commitment to counseling. As in many preparation programs, "counseling" includes the nuts and bolts of the college application process: tests, deadlines and personal essays. But NAI also seeks to address the social and emotional issues often associated with adolescence. In particular, NAI seeks to address the problems often confronted when students grow up in low-income, urban areas. The dangers of drugs, gangs, unemployment and violence are frequently topics of conversation. If students are going to learn and thrive, they must deal proactively with such problems, NAI program staff believe. When teachers note problems with particular students, counselors are quick to respond; when students have difficulties at home, they talk about them with program counselors; when students have conflicts with parents or peers, they meet with program counselors. Students have pointed to the assistance provided by the program, but also to the demands of participation: NAI has been referred to as a "loving boot camp" that requires discipline and supports each individual (Tierney and Jun 2001:213). Further, NAI staff connect culture to the counseling process, recognizing that students' lives are contextually situated; academic, familial and emotional problems develop in specific settings and require specific tools for resolution.

Student and family investments in the NAI program are significant, and so are the rewards. Students who persist from seventh to twelfth grade and who meet specific criteria for admission at USC receive full scholarships from the university. Once settled on the USC campus as college freshmen, NAI students receive support from a university program administered through the Center for Academic Support. Advisers associated with the center provide academic counseling, connection to faculty and staff in specific majors, and career advising. When needed, center advisers can also recommend tutors or study groups. More generally, center advisers offer social and emotional support; many students visit the office weekly to study, speak with advisers or connect with friends.

Students who do not meet criteria for admission as freshmen have additional options: they can complete coursework at a community college and transfer to USC after two years. At the time of transfer, the full scholarship is available. Financial assistance is also available while students are enrolled in two-year schools. Students who earn admission to other four-year schools also have the option of returning to USC as graduate students. Scholarships are available for two years of graduate studies.

The description above provides specific information about NAI program operations. Several program characteristics that support success are clear: the duration of the program, beginning with students at a critical educational moment and supporting them throughout high school; intensive academic training including Saturday and summer workshops, test preparation, and enriched coursework in writing and mathematics; family and community engagement; and a partnership with the university aimed at supporting students through their baccalaureate degrees.

The following sections of this chapter will discuss NAI's causes for celebration over the past 15 years and also the challenges NAI faces in the years ahead. Then the theoretical framework that guides the program will be explained, in particular, the concepts of cultural capital and cultural integrity. The chapter will conclude with lessons learned from NAI that may guide the next generation of college preparatory programs.

Program Challenges and Celebrations

The successes of NAI are pronounced and sensational. Students have been featured in local and national news reports, campus magazine articles and regional newspaper stories. *Time/Princeton Review College Guide* featured the program in a 2000 article describing USC's campus outreach (Hornblower 2000). The partnership between NAI and the university is remarkable as each commits significant time, space and resources. Perhaps most importantly, cohorts of students have graduated from the program and have gone on to successful college careers—at USC as well as at other public, private, two- and four-year schools. Since the program began graduating students in 1997, an average of 43 percent of the graduates have gone on to study at USC. Of the 44 students who graduated from high school in 2001, 23 percent attend USC, 9 percent are enrolled in the University of California system, 23 percent are at a California State University school, and 15 percent are at other four-year private schools. The remainder of the students enrolled at community colleges with the expectation that they will transfer to four-year schools. Perhaps most importantly, each of the 44 graduates matriculated to postsecondary study after completing the NAI program. And now that a generation of program participants have graduated from college, alumni have returned to mentor younger students. Many alumni have continued into graduate studies after being first in their families to graduate from college. The past 15 years, however, have not always been easy. This section outlines some of the challenges and celebrations the program has welcomed and endured. Like most programs, NAI has continued to evolve as new students enter the program and new graduating classes move into college.

Celebrations

Angelica stood at the crosswalk with a group of young students, waiting for the light to change. Across the street is the Natural History Museum, and she has been charged with accompanying the small group of

NAI eighth graders on the field trip. While waiting, they talked about living in the residence halls at USC and the cost of college textbooks. "My parents," she explained, "they didn't want me to live on campus. You know, they're...they just wanted me to live at home. I don't know how (my counselor) convinced them." Angelica, herself an NAI graduate, recently completed her master's degree in history and joined the doctoral program last fall. She wants to be a college professor.

Each year, as a new cohort of students graduates from NAI and moves into college, the program has more alumni to call on for mentoring and for stories of inspiration. Each year, more NAI alumni also graduate from college, fulfilling the promise of the program and the dreams of their families. These are the celebrations that are easiest to identify, but there are others. One of the most important outcomes of NAI has been the continued partnership developed between USC and the local Los Ángeles high schools. The partnership connects the university to the community in tangible ways and takes advantage of the living laboratory in the school's front yard. This partnership is particularly important as educators, politicians and citizens seek more equitable educational opportunities for children. Though NAI is a small program—one requiring a significant financial investment—the principles of cultural affirmation and local identities are transferable to other college preparation models.

Another important aspect of the program's success is family involvement. While parents and guardians engage in the students' education in significant ways, they also prepare themselves emotionally and financially to send their children off to college. Just as students need support and assistance in college-going, so do families. Again, the result is infectious. Families and NAI students, in turn, support younger relatives and neighbors. By reaching out to families, NAI also reaches into the surrounding community.

Challenges

Johnnie sat at a table on the third floor of the library. Over his calculus textbook, he gazed out the window to the patio below, where students laughed over late-night coffee and relaxed—a short study break—on the concrete steps. He had completed calculus as a high school student, but he struggled with the college course. "It's like I didn't even do this before," he sighed. The next morning, Johnnie would sit for his first college midterm, and he was anxious. He turned from the window and resumed his careful studying. Three weeks later, Johnnie dropped the course.

Johnnie's struggle with calculus reflects a particular kind of program challenge: the individual student's academic challenges. While these are significant and pressing, other difficulties have surfaced through the years. This section discusses program as well as student challenges. Because some of the administrative challenges are instructive and may be useful for program developers, they are discussed in some detail.

Program location. The main office for NAI is located in a university annex, across a busy street from the main campus. In a strip mall called "UV" (University Village), the office is next door to a sandwich shop and a fast-food noodle restaurant. This location is not the original; indeed, the program's move into the strip mall followed a number of years of debate: Where should the program be housed? the provost's office? the USC Rossier School of Education? the Office of Community Outreach? Though the office location is a seemingly benign question, it points to one of the greatest challenges of the program. Since its beginning, NAI has been searching for a home on the university campus. This search also points to additional program challenges including staffing, funding and evaluation.

One of the strengths of the NAI program is in the commitment evidenced by students, families, program staff and the university community. Commitment from the university—money as well as classroom space—is of central importance. When USC and NAI first developed a partnership, NAI was housed under USC's office of the provost, an office that holds distinction and suggests a weight of commitment. As at many universities, however, the level of financial and staff support was difficult to maintain. The program was relocated to another office space, though still under the auspices of the provost. Still later, university officials struggled with where better to house the project, and looked into pairing the program with the university's Rossier School of Education. Ultimately, the partnership did not materialize, and the program was moved to the off-campus location.

Geography on college campuses is important; the controversy over the program's location provides a salient example. Many gestures can be used to exemplify the university's support of the program, and the problem of location should not be misunderstood as an act of dismissal. The relocation of the program was inspired by questions of physical space—a commodity in short supply in all university buildings. The current location of the office, however, suggests disconnection between the programs, despite the intricate partnership cultivated over the years. Communication is more difficult because of location, which affects all aspects of the program to some degree. For example, conversations with the university office of admissions—an important line of communication as juniors and seniors prepare applications—is hampered by the distance. Perhaps most importantly, the office location pulls students off campus, away from classrooms and teachers, where they need to seek assistance. Likewise, program administrators are distanced from the day-to-day activities of the students.

In addition to practical matters of communication and distance, NAI's office location is problematic in terms of inclusion in the campus community. A program such as NAI—serving low-income, urban minority students—is by definition serving students on the margins of higher education. Though the message is subtle, the office location mirrors that marginalization in real terms. Such a message is out of place given the university's investment in and commitment to NAI.

Program timing. One of the more material challenges for NAI relates to program design. While ample research on college preparation programs points to the importance of early interventions and long-term support (Allen and Bonous-Hammarth 2004), this presents a problem in urban areas. Students and families are asked to dedicate a significant amount of time to the program, both in terms of daily activities and years of participation. As in many large urban centers, Los Angeles residents tend to be transient. Families move into different neighborhoods and cities because of job or housing opportunities. These changes in students' lives complicate participation, sometimes making program continuation impossible.

The length of the program, however, is far more often an aspect of celebration than of challenge. Students and families grow into close cohorts, and program staff get to know each student well. Students develop a sense of belonging, of being one of the "NAI Scholars," in schools where academic achievement is not always recognized or valued. NAI students receive considerable help preparing for college-level work and entrance exams. College-going is a complex journey, and the duration of the NAI program allows students and families to approach each step with support and guidance.

Funding and resources. Partnership with USC provides NAI with many resources: Students not only benefit from the material resources of the campus (space for weekday classes and Saturday programs, tutoring by USC students, and libraries), they also benefit spiritually. One student noted, "I like coming here...you know, you get to be at college while you're still at high school." The setting provides a sense of accomplishment and allows students to become familiar with the campus; students develop important social and cultural capital just by virtue of interacting within the environment (Tierney and Jun 2001). (The role of social and cultural capital in NAI will be discussed in more detail later.)

In an era of decreasing budgets and increasing costs, program funding is an almost constant issue. NAI is a nonprofit organization that depends on public, private and corporate funding for all aspects of program implementation. The university provides a great deal of in-kind and material support, but NAI must also apply for grants in order to keep the program operational. Administrators, teachers, tutors, counselors, supplies and academic resources—all are essential aspects of program success, and all require significant financial resources.

NAI has had a great deal of success securing funding, but administrators note that the process is continuous. If they could secure additional funds, a full-time development officer would be hired (Tierney, Hagedorn, and Colyar 2002). Staffing restrictions also limit the amount of evaluation the program can reasonably accomplish—data collection is time consuming and difficult; the program has not always had resources dedicated to updating program files and student contact information. As a result, longitudinal data are not consistent, and sometimes are not available. High school graduation rates, college enrollment figures and college persistence data for NAI students are not routinely updated. Such data could be helpful in grant applications as the program seeks continued support.

Student challenges: Academics. Over the six years of the program, students face a number of challenges, both social and academic. Because of the time commitments of the program, it is difficult for students to work while they are in high school, and they often do not have time for co-curricular activities. And because they are at the college campus for part of the day, they do not have the same connection to their high school "home" as other students might. The most pressing challenges, however, come when NAI students transition into their postsecondary settings. Despite years of college preparation, the first semesters are difficult.

NAI students are sometimes underprepared for the rigors of college coursework. Grades from high school are often considered inflated, so a student's grade point average (GPA), often exceeding 4.0, does not represent an accurate portrait of his or her skills. A student like Johnnie, who received an "A" in Advanced Placement Calculus, for example, might do very poorly in a college calculus class. With the demands on students' time, particularly when students are working part-time, many struggle to maintain their college GPAs.

Beginning in the seventh grade, NAI students are called "Scholars" and are encouraged by the significant human resources of the community, program and USC partners. Most enroll in a number of Advanced Placement courses, and many earn top grades in their high school graduating classes. When they enter their freshmen year in college, however, they are part of a cohort considered academically "at risk." NAI students are required to enroll in a support program called the Structured Curriculum Program, which is required of all students who do not meet the requirements for "regular" admission. (SAT scores and GPA admission requirements for the NAI Scholars are lower than the average admission scores for incoming freshmen.) Suddenly, the NAI Scholars are at the bottom of the academic heap, and they are surrounded by some of the most competitive and high-achieving students in the nation. For many, this creates frustration, anger and confusion— they are not used to facing coursework they cannot complete (Tierney, Hagedorn, and Colyar 2002). In some cases, the courses they excelled in during high school seem like foreign languages (Colyar 2002).

Although these challenges are clearly academic, they are also psychologically troubling and can complicate the experiences of these students. At the same time, the counseling and support systems they have grown accustomed to in the NAI program are no longer as easily available, if they are available at all. NAI students have access to the many programs and support services available to the campus community, but many of the students do not know where, how and when to access help (Colyar 2002).

Student challenges: Social. The transition into college can also be socially challenging. Though NAI students have been coming to the USC campus for six years, they sometimes have difficulty "fitting in" when they arrive as freshmen. They have attended high schools with predominantly African American and Latino/a students, and they are unaccustomed to the diversity present on the USC campus. One NAI student noted, "I've never been in a class with a white person before." In addition, NAI students must transition into large classes, some with an enrollment of 100 or more. They are used to a great deal of contact with faculty and program staff—teachers and counselors who follow their progress closely and intervene when necessary. They have been surrounded by the same cohort of students for many years, and have come to rely on familiarity as a form of comfort. In the new college setting, classes are larger and less intimate, lecture halls seem full of strangers, and faculty are not always attentive to individual student needs.

As more students graduate from the program and enroll at USC and other schools, NAI administrators continue to refine support programs aimed at easing student transitions into college. The close partnership between NAI and USC staff make this effort possible, again emphasizing the importance of collaboration across the community.

Connecting Culture

The descriptions above provide specific information about the NAI program—celebrations and challenges. This section discusses the theoretical framework that guides NAI, in particular the concepts of cultural capital and cultural integrity.

Cultural Capital

For many years, educators and researchers have used the notions of capital developed by Pierre Bourdieu (1977, 1986) to frame discussions about how social class shapes educational achievement. Bourdieu (1986:243) distinguishes between three types of capital:

- *Economic capital,* that is, money and material objects used to produce goods and services (Turner 1991:512). In the educational context, this might equate to scholarships covering tuition and books for classes.
- *Social capital,* that is, positions and relations in social networks (Turner 1991:512). An example drawn from a college preparatory program might be getting to know admissions staff and faculty members at a university as people who can facilitate a student's acceptance into that institution.
- *Cultural capital,* that is, informal interpersonal skills and abilities that legitimate the maintenance of status and power. This last form of capital, cultural capital, is the one most relevant to NAI; thus, it will be discussed in some detail.

Cultural capital can be imagined as one element of individual contexts; it is a concept that attempts to name abstract cultural knowledge that influences one's academic success. In Bourdieu's definition, cultural capital is transmitted from one generation to the next, such that families of high status pass on the information needed to maintain that status to future generations. Transmission is not necessarily deliberate; it may be entirely unconscious, passed along in practices that are part of a family or community's standard repertoire.

Additional scholars have since defined cultural capital in different ways. Patricia McDonough (1997:9) offers a simpler definition: "the knowledge that social elites value yet schools do not teach." Thus, cultural capital is significant in terms of educational achievement. Families from middle and upper classes are privileged in terms of economic security, educational aspiration and support systems; these families possess the resources and knowledge needed to help their children go to college. Families without sufficient cultural capital regarding schooling are educationally disadvantaged; young people without resources and knowledge may self-select out of the college track or lower their educational goals. In addition, without the explicit knowledge of the benefits that come with postsecondary education, a student might not be motivated to persist and invest the necessary time and effort.

Cultural capital is a complex idea in its connection to structures of status and power, but these definitions at least provide a vocabulary for thinking about college access. Students like Johnnie, Tiffanie and Angelica come to their educational experiences with different cultural capital than those who attend elite private schools or schools located in affluent suburbs, that is, schools with different demographics. One of NAI's goals is to bring these students and their families into contact with different forms of capital, different resources and different opportunities that translate into new understandings and aspirations.

Preparation programs like NAI can connect students to networks that may be helpful in developing the social capital necessary for college success. These networks may offer psychological or emotional support; they also might provide opportunities for internships or after-school jobs. NAI also provides the economic capital necessary for college success, in the form of full scholarships to USC.

Bourdieu's notions of capital are problematic, however, because defined in this manner, they point to a "deficiency" in the experiences of minority families. So defined, Bourdieu's notions of capital suggest that there are practices and values necessary for academic success that Latino/a and African American families do not possess. While NAI recognizes that there are skills underrepresented students need in order to become academically prepared for college, the program also acknowledges the value of cultural practices families already possess. Rather than seek to remedy a cultural deficiency, NAI combines the concept of cultural capital with a second concept, that of cultural integrity.

Cultural Integrity

Research by Daphna Oyserman, described in Chapter One, suggests that "students with...complex self-concepts were significantly more likely than their peers to perform well on school tasks" (Glenn 2003).

Students with "complex self-concepts" have positive beliefs about their specific ethnic groups and some engagement with the society at large. Students with complex self-concepts do not attempt to assimilate completely into the dominant culture, but maintain a sense of positive ethnic identity.

Oyserman's work points at one of the philosophical foundations of NAI: At the heart of the program is an attention to cultural integrity. Student success cannot be fully realized by teaching academic skills and preparing students for entrance exams. These elements are important, but they are not sufficient. College preparation is a complex task that requires skill development as well as personal growth. For African American and Latino/a students, such identity development occurs in particular contexts. The NAI program uses these contexts—educational settings as well as family and community settings—as rich sites of cultural practice. Rather than asking students to abandon their family and cultural ties, NAI encourages students to celebrate them and develop "complex self-concepts." NAI students do not cultivate a new form of cultural capital in favor of their own. Instead, NAI works toward developing *Latino/a* Scholars and *African American* Scholars, not just students prepared to enter college. Indeed, race and ethnicity matter in the NAI program.

The term "cultural integrity" comes from Donna Deyhle's ten-year ethnographic study of Navajo youth (Deyhle 1995), also discussed in Chapter One. Deyhle found that Navajo students who were more secure in their traditional culture were more likely to have academic success. The successful Navajo students did not assimilate into the larger white culture; they cultivated their academic talents while also maintaining ties to the Navajo community. Tierney and Jun (2001) further define "cultural integrity" as:

> programs and teaching strategies that call upon students' racial and ethnic backgrounds in a positive manner in the development of their pedagogies and learning activities. Cultural integrity removes the problem from the child and looks on the child's background neither as neutral nor a negative factor

for learning. Instead, the adolescent's cultural background is a critical ingredi-
ent for acquiring cultural capital and achieving success. (P. 211)

This definition recognizes the importance of both cultural capital and
cultural integrity in working toward success for students of color.

Work by Claude Steele (1997) on stereotype threat is also useful
to mention again in a discussion of cultural integrity. Stereotypes,
Steele notes, can positively or negatively influence academic performance. For example, a Latino/a student who performs poorly on an
assignment is stereotyped as "lazy," an assessment that may be based
on nothing more than racial background. The label may then be used
by the student to predict or justify the next bad grade. The stereotype
becomes "self-relevant," sometimes before a student even steps into a
classroom. Breaking out of the stereotype, a process Steele (1997:614)
refers to as "disidentification," is seen as a turning away from family
and community and striving for something typically associated with
Anglo students. NAI emphasizes high achievement as a characteristic
that cuts across cultures and ethnic groups. All students are "Scholars,"
and all are expected to do well.

Lessons Learned

Tiffanie's mother had to take off work so that she could attend the
graduation. She dressed carefully and chose a hat to shade her face
from the bright sun; by the time the ceremony was over, it would be
after 1 p.m. Mr. and Mrs. Morgan and Tiffanie's sister, Janet, were
eating a hurried breakfast when the phone rang. Tiffanie was calling.
"Don't forget the camera," she reminded them. "And will you bring
me a bottle of water?" "The bag is packed," Mrs. Morgan laughed. "We
know, we've got the camera, and we've got the water. We'll see you in
a few minutes."

The success of NAI depends on the dedication of several important
stakeholders: students, families, teachers, NAI staff and the university. These partnerships are important as students look toward their
futures. Partnerships make financial aid, in the form of full-tuition
scholarships, possible. Partnerships smooth the admissions process.
They also leverage the human resources of the university, local schools
and students' communities. Students are encouraged to work together
on their coursework. Teachers and families work together to develop
student intellect and self-concept. The importance of culture is evident
in the delicate balance of actors who work together to move students
toward academic success. NAI has developed a culture of collaboration

and inclusion to support all of the larger aims of the program.

Clearly, NAI is expensive and relies on a number of moving parts. Different universities may partner with college preparation programs in different ways. The description of NAI included in this chapter illustrates the importance of programs shaping themselves to local needs.

Several of NAI's principles are useful in thinking about college preparation and ethnicity more generally. The following section provides a summary of recommendations that may serve to inspire the next generation of college preparation programs.

Partnerships help ensure success. One of the most important elements of NAI's program is in the partnership with the university; similarly, partnerships with families and local communities are essential. Such partnerships enable resource sharing and a common investment—all partners can share in the success of helping students get to college.

College preparation takes time. Not all programs have the luxury of six years of preparation. The complexity of college preparation does demand a commitment more substantial than the final semester or year of high school. Early interventions with sustained activities help ensure student success.

Evaluation is important. As NAI program administrators continue to struggle for sustained funding and a central location on the USC campus, evaluation still takes a back seat. However, evaluation, including longitudinal research, is an essential activity that will provide much-needed data for potential funding agencies. Evaluation also will provide insights into program strengths and weaknesses.

Support is necessary even after students enroll in college. NAI students are well equipped to enter postsecondary education, but they continue to need academic and social support. College preparation programs should look ahead to the college years, and specific strategies should be developed that provide sustained assistance. As part of the NAI's culture of achievement, teachers and program staff should emphasize the importance of seeking help so that when students enter college, they are comfortable working with tutors, faculty and peers.

Family engagement is important for student success. Far too often families are excluded from students' educational experiences because of time constraints or language barriers. Parents and guardians are powerful allies, and their participation benefits all concerned.

Culture is an integral part of program—and student—success. This
final point is perhaps the most important aspect of NAI's philosophy
and implementation. Emphasizing and celebrating culture means
meeting students in their own contexts and affirming the value of their
experiences. While specific behaviors might be added to their stores,
these do not replace those of the family and the community.

References

Allen, Walter and Marguerite Bonous-Hammarth. 2004. "A Dream Deferred: The Critical Factor of Timing in College Preparation and Outreach." Pp. 155–172 in *Preparing for College: Nine Elements of Effective Outreach*, edited by W. Tierney, Z. Corwin, and J. Colyar. Albany: State University of New York Press.

Bourdieu, Pierre. 1977. "Cultural Reproduction and Social Reproduction." Pp. 487–511 in *Power and Ideology in Education*, edited by J. Karabel and A. H. Halsey. New York: Oxford University Press.

———. 1986. "The Forms of Capital." Pp. 241–258 in *Handbook of Theory and Research for the Sociology of Education*, edited by J. G. Richardson. New York: Greenwood Press.

Colyar, Julia. 2002. "Listening to Student Stories: A Narrative Ethnography of Minority Students in the First Year of College." Ph.D. dissertation, Rossier School of Education, University of Southern California, Los Angeles, Calif.

Deyhle, Donna. 1995. "Navajo Youth and Anglo Racism: Cultural Integrity and Resistance." *Harvard Educational Review* 65:403–444.

Glenn, David. 2003, June 2. "Minority Students With Complex Beliefs About Ethnic Identity Are Found to Do Better in School." *The Chronicle of Higher Education*. Retrieved July 17, 2003, from http://chronicle.com/daily/2003/06/2003060201n.htm

Horn, Laura and Xianglei Chen. 1998. *Toward Resiliency: At-Risk Students Who Make it to College*. Washington, D.C.: Office of Educational Research and Improvement, U.S. Department of Education.

Hornblower, Margot. 2000. "The Gown Goes to Town." *Time/Princeton Review College Guide*. August 23:71–77.

McDonough, Patricia. 1997. *Choosing Colleges: How Social Class and Schools Structure Opportunity*. Albany: State University of New York Press.

Neighborhood Academic Initiative. (1999, March 19). *Purpose*. Retrieved December 21, 2004, from http://www.usc.edu/admin/provost/nai/nai.html

Steele, Claude M. 1997. "A Threat in the Air: How Stereotypes Shape Intellectual Identity and Performance." *American Psychologist* 52:613–629.

Tierney, William G. and Alexander Jun. 2001. "A University Helps Prepare Low Income Youths for College: Tracking School Success." *The Journal of Higher Education* 72:205–225.

Tierney, William G., Linda Hagedorn, and Julia Colyar. 2002. *Students of*

College Preparation Programs in Postsecondary Institutions: Improving Program Effectiveness and Student Achievement. Los Angeles: Center for Higher Education Policy Analysis, University of Southern California.

Turner, Jonathan H. 1991. *The Structure of Sociological Theory.* Belmont, Calif.: Wadsworth Publishing Company.

3

2+2+2: An Equation for Native American Student Success

Tim Nichols and Laurie Stenberg Nichols

The 2+2+2 project is a collaborative effort between educational institutions in South Dakota to help more of the state's Native American students complete baccalaureate degrees in the agricultural, biological, family and consumer sciences. Headquartered at South Dakota State University (SDSU) in the College of Agriculture and Biological Sciences and the College of Family and Consumer Sciences, the program also involves tribal colleges and reservation high schools working together to meet this challenge. Each "two" of the 2+2+2 represents two years: first, two years at a reservation high school; second, two years at a tribal college; and finally, two years at SDSU. Thus, the program aims to build "an educational ladder with every rung in place" for Native American students. The program's long-range goal is to develop resident expertise among American Indians on South Dakota reservations, so that these communities will be better equipped to face the challenges confronting them.

This chapter will provide background information on the project's context, an overview of 2+2+2's multifaceted approach and a discussion of how ethnicity matters in 2+2+2. Several barriers to success will be discussed as well as several catalysts for change. Finally, the philosophical scaffolding that supports 2+2+2 will be reviewed in some detail.

2+2+2—Background and Context

With any educational program, understanding the context and issues it is designed to address is important. D. Michael Pavel and colleagues

summed up the status of American Indian education like this: despite
recent gains, including increased access to higher education (particularly for American Indian women and particularly at the tribal
colleges), many factors continue to act as barriers to American Indians'
access to higher education. Native people continue to suffer from a
traumatic legacy, which has included boarding schools and economic,
educational, cultural and spiritual oppression (Pavel et al. 1998). Barriers for American Indians to higher education today include isolation
(Wax, Wax, and Dumont 1964; American Indian Higher Education
Consortium 1999), poverty (Carter 1999), poor academic preparation,
unsupportive educational environments, institutional racism (Feagin,
Hernan, and Imani 1996) and cultural discontinuity between Native
communities and mainstream higher education institutions (Huffman
1999; St. Germaine 1995; Wright and Tierney 1991). As a result, there
is a continued gap in educational attainment between Indians and
non-Indians. American Indians lag behind other U.S. ethnic minority
groups in many measures of educational attainment (Harvey 2001;
Pavel et al. 1998).

For South Dakota—with Native Americans constituting almost 10
percent of the population and with 20 percent of the state's land mass
located on one of nine Indian reservations—issues of American Indian
education are critical to the state's well-being. Underscoring this issue
is the relative youth of the state's American Indian population. In 1995,
approximately 12 percent of the nation's Native American children
resided in South Dakota (*Kids Count Data Book* 1997), whereas on several
South Dakota reservations nearly half of the population is under the
age of 18 (Baer, Arwood, and Spencer 1994). Furthermore, instances of
poverty, unemployment and fetal alcohol syndrome on South Dakota
reservations are among the nation's highest. Educational realities are
also harsh; many young Native Americans drop out of school, and
enrollment in postsecondary education is less than one percent (Boyer
1997).

A bright spot on the landscape of American Indian education in the
last 30 years has been the establishment and growth of tribal colleges. A
manifestation of the drive for self-determination among Native people,
the tribal college movement began in the late 1960s and in the years
since has improved the educational and economic status of American
Indians in higher education (Boyer 1997; Oppelt 1990; Stein 1992; Szasz
1999). Nationwide, enrollment at tribal colleges has grown from approximately 2,100 undergraduates in 1982 to 24,363 undergraduates
and 250 graduate students in 1996. In states with tribal colleges, the

proportion of American Indian students being educated therein rose 62 percent between 1990 and 1996. Enrollment growth has been accompanied by expanded academic offerings, so that several tribal colleges now offer baccalaureate and graduate degrees, in addition to associate degrees and certificate programs (American Indian Higher Education Consortium 1999; Stein 1992). Currently, of the nation's 32 tribal colleges, five are located in South Dakota. (They are Si Tanka University, Lower Brule Community College, Oglala Lakota College, Sinte Gleska University and Sisseton Wahpeton College.) The proportion of South Dakota American Indian college students attending tribal colleges rose from 22 percent in 1978 to 70 percent ten years later (Tierney 1992).

Though initially modeled after and similar in many ways to mainstream community colleges, tribal colleges have a unique (Oppelt 1990; Stein 1992), explicit mission to explore, rebuild and/or reinforce tribal cultures using curricula and institutional settings that are conducive to the success of American Indians (American Indian Higher Education Consortium 1999). W. Larry Belgarde (1993) suggests that tribal colleges can be a bridge between their Indian clientele and the larger academic society. Margaret Szasz (1999) describes how tribal colleges have become "cultural intermediaries" for American Indian college students, reaffirming their Native identity and providing training for survival in the contemporary world.

Still, tribal colleges remain mostly small, two-year institutions, often located on relatively remote Indian reservations and aimed at meeting the educational needs of particular tribal communities. Of those students who do attend tribal colleges, many do not complete their associate degrees, and in South Dakota, very few transfer on to four-year baccalaureate programs. Among the small share who do enroll at four-year institutions off-reservation, many face barriers to success that prove insurmountable.

Meanwhile, demographic shifts, accreditation requirements and a fuller appreciation of what it means to be an "engaged institution" (W. K. Kellogg Foundation 1999) have led many mainstream universities to emphasize diversity and outreach to the ethnic minority communities in their states (Tierney 1993, 1998).

Numerous scholars (Baird 1996; Boyer 1997; McDonald 2000; Nichols, Baird, and Kayongo-Male 2001) have called on state universities to work collaboratively with tribal institutions to more effectively serve American Indian constituents. The 2+2+2 program represents an organic, systemic attempt to partner across educational levels and answer this call.

What Is 2+2+2?

The 2+2+2 project is a broad umbrella program involving faculty, staff, students and community members at about 15 reservation high schools, five tribal colleges and SDSU, working to ensure smooth transitions for Native American students between educational institutions. The goal is to help these students complete their baccalaureate degrees and to return to reservation communities as professionals in the agricultural, biological, family and consumer sciences. Tribal colleges are an integral part of the equation. Allowing students to remain in their home communities and begin their coursework at tribal colleges makes the transition to the four-year university more successful. This model supports the work of Linda Pertusati (1988) who found that Native American students who spent some years of their education in all-Native classrooms where culture was reinforced (like reservation high schools and tribal colleges) developed a stronger sense of ethnic identity and were more successful later in classrooms that were dominated by white students.

Nested within the 2+2+2 project are six primary clusters of activity: articulation agreements, experiential learning, curriculum development, distance education, student support and faculty development. Each of these activities is described below.

Articulation Agreements

Agreements that ensure equitable credit transfer between the institutions involved are critical to collaborative success. Students moving between reservation high schools, tribal colleges and SDSU need assurance that their credits will receive fair evaluation at each level. Project efforts have negotiated course-by-course equivalencies between participating tribal colleges and SDSU. In addition, discipline faculty have developed specific transfer guides for tribal students that describe courses of study needed at each level. This has involved an intensive planning process between faculty at high schools, tribal colleges and SDSU. Coordinated course offerings and course numbering all have been considered in developing the transfer guides. Transfer guides help students plan for their future in an informed, purposeful manner and further ease the transition from high school to tribal college and from tribal college to SDSU.

Experiential Learning

Like many high school students in South Dakota, most American Indians do not have a clear picture of the career opportunities available to them in agriculture and biological sciences and in family and consumer sciences (Nichols and Nichols 1998). A key thrust of the 2+2+2 project aims to provide these students with hands-on learning opportunities that will motivate them to pursue careers in one of these disciplines. In a sense, 2+2+2 allows students important opportunities to "try on" different *professional* American Indian identities (Lal 1995) such as "I can be a Native American dietician" or "I can be a Native American wildlife biologist."

Sample approaches have included a research apprenticeship program that brings Native high school and tribal college students to SDSU each summer for several weeks of research with faculty scientists. An annual three-day 2+2+2 summer institute offers approximately 30 American Indian students a shorter but still meaningful dose of experiential learning. An action-oriented approach has proven most successful for engaging institute participants. Sample summer workshops have focused on topics such as aquatic biology, tissue culture, Geographic Information Systems, early childhood education sensory activities, nutrient analysis and the integration of Native American cultural symbolism into interior design. The institute program also includes sessions on college and career planning, panel discussions with current American Indian students and 2+2+2 alumni, and keynote addresses by prominent tribal leaders. Reservation high school and tribal college teachers help plan, organize and staff the institute, in addition to serving as local promoters and recruiters for the program.

The 2+2+2 experiential learning programs are designed to foster career awareness in a culturally relevant context. Participants are repeatedly informed of how an education and career in agricultural, biological, family and consumer sciences can lead to reservation employment.

Curriculum Development

Curriculum lies at the heart of students' academic experience. Because it is important for American Indian students to see their culture reflected in curriculum (Huffman 1999), small grants are provided for SDSU faculty to integrate Native American perspectives into course offerings. Courses that have been revised for inclusion of Native perspectives include biology, arboriculture, crop production, range management, soils, food principles, family relations and gerontology. Andrew

Garrod and Colleen Larimore (1997) describe how such courses, along with classes in American Indian studies, can enhance Native students' ethnic identity and inculcate feelings of pride and empowerment among American Indian students.

Several SDSU and tribal college faculty are also revising their courses to include collaborative learning experiences for students. For example, forestry instructors at SDSU and Sinte Gleska University have taken their students on a joint field trip to South Dakota's Black Hills where they engaged in hands-on forestry and held campfire discussions around topics such as the ethics of clear-cutting and the spiritual significance of the Black Hills to the Lakota people. SDSU and Oglala Lakota College horticulture students have teamed with high schools on the Pine Ridge reservation for design and installation of landscaping projects at local elementary schools. Agribusiness students in SDSU's Small Business Management class have worked with their tribal college counterparts on the Rosebud reservation, acting as consultants for economic feasibility studies of proposed agricultural enterprises. Early childhood education students have worked together in Head Start classrooms on reservations in Flandreau and Sisseton. While being valuable experiences for tribal participants, these programs also serve to raise the sensitivity, awareness and cultural competency of SDSU students and faculty as well.

Distance Education

Because many American Indian students are place-bound, 2+2+2 efforts have taken courses to them. Distance education has provided college courses to remote sites through technology, such as interactive television and Internet. As a supplement to technology-based distance education efforts, the 2+2+2 has sponsored short courses on reservations designed to enhance collaborative activity between SDSU and tribal college faculty, to strengthen the project's presence in tribal communities, and to build relations with interested American Indian students.

Student Support

A primary aim of the 2+2+2 is to provide support for students as they move between educational levels. For many American Indians, these transitions can be equated to culture shock (Garrod and Larimore 1997). While the 2+2+2 is designed to ease this transition, it remains difficult for American Indian students to leave their reservation homes and extended families. Transitions are further complicated because many

American Indian students graduate from high school underprepared for the academic rigors of college life (Huffman 1999). The tribal colleges' noble efforts to accommodate students' needs should be applauded, though extra effort is needed on all fronts to help students transition to the more academically competitive state university environment. Close connections to academic advisers and other campus resource people have proven critical to student success.

Because of high levels of poverty among American Indian students in South Dakota, financial aid is another critical piece of student support (Baer, Arwood, and Spencer 1994). In addition to a generous scholarship program for students in their final two years of the 2+2+2, students are paid for their involvement in undergraduate research projects in their areas of interest. The 2+2+2 program also assists students with families by waiving their children's tuition at the SDSU Laboratory Pre-School (Nichols and Nichols 1998).

Garrod and Larimore (1997) describe the importance of American Indians finding a sense of community with fellow students. Henry Trueba and Yali Zou (1994) argue that strong ethnic identity, sense of community and social support can help minority students overcome barriers to success. To help create support networks, 2+2+2 students visit SDSU and interact with American Indian students and staff. SDSU's Native American Club and Native American student adviser help to host visiting students, provide free tutoring once students enroll on campus and invite them to participate in activities such as the annual SDSU American Indian History and Culture Conference and the *Wacipi* (pow-wow). In addition, 2+2+2 students are encouraged to get involved with organizations related to their academic fields of study. Intensive, culturally sensitive orientation activities also have been developed. The personal relationship between Native American students and campus resource people, built through sustained interaction over time, has helped contribute to individual student success as well as to long-term project success.

Faculty Development

Early in the project, SDSU staff realized that to effectively partner with tribal educators and serve tribal students, they needed to learn more about tribal culture. The project invested in supporting faculty travel to the reservations, buying books and materials, and bringing speakers to campus—all aimed at helping SDSU faculty better understand Native history and culture. The 2+2+2 program sponsored summer visits for faculty to the state's reservations, tribal high schools and colleges, tribal employers, Native American alumni, and important cultural sites. Most faculty participating in the visits (up to 20 per year) had not previously visited the state's reservations. Learning about these places and their people quite literally helped SDSU faculty better understand where their Native American students were coming from. In addition, the visits helped faculty connect with colleagues who shared similar or complementary academic interests. This paved the way for future collaboration. Faculty development also evolved into a more reciprocal relationship over time. This included bringing graduate coursework to the reservations and sponsoring SDSU faculty as exchange professors on the tribal college campuses.

How Ethnicity Matters in 2+2+2

With this overview of the project, the next section addresses the central issue at the heart of this volume—how and why does ethnicity matter? Ethnicity is, in fact, reflected throughout the 2+2+2 program. Joane Nagel (1994) uses the metaphor of the shopping cart to describe how a minority student can pick and choose cultural items to construct an ethnic identity that will best serve that student in a given situation. Implicit in 2+2+2 programming is the aim to help American Indian students choose items wisely for their shopping carts. Extensive effort has been made to integrate American Indian cultural perspectives throughout the program's activities.

Project Origins

Ethnicity mattered with 2+2+2 at the very beginning of the project in 1995. Critical to all the project's future activity was the fact that the initial request for collaboration came from American Indian people—tribal college staff came to the university seeking a partnership program that would help more of their students complete baccalaureate degrees. After learning of this, during the early weeks and months of the project, staff from SDSU traveled to four of the state's reservations to visit with high school and tribal college faculty, students and community leaders about their hopes and dreams for the new endeavor. These individuals had substantive input into shaping the project's direction. A significant factor in the evolution of the project was the fact that university staff members "went there"—to the reservation communities—investing time, energy and finances so that they might listen and establish relationships with potential project partners. This follows the advice of Cheryl Crazy Bull (1997) for non-Native collaborators to establish close, personal and enduring relationships among tribal people. Any collaborative effort, she suggests, should have tangible benefits for the tribal community.

Project Goals

It quickly became apparent in formative discussions about project goals that 2+2+2 would be different from existing university recruitment efforts. Most college preparatory programs seek to help students graduate from high school and enroll in the higher education institution of their choosing. Indeed, SDSU participants initially envisioned the project with this approach in mind. Early conversations at planning meetings on three different reservations, however, pointed to an alternative measure of student success. Reservation high school and tribal college faculty and staff sought to have their young people not only succeed educationally and professionally, but also to return to their home (or other reservation) communities prepared to meet the challenges facing Native people today. Tribal educators spoke passionately about the need for Native American young people to not simply "get rich and contribute to the white man's world," but rather to return and to serve their own. This is in keeping with the discussion by Garrod and Larimore (1997) of "completing the circle"—the desire among many college-educated American Indians to apply their knowledge and skills in ways that will make a difference for their people.

Local voices also helped shape academic areas of emphasis for the 2+2+2. Originally planned to emphasize agriculture and natural resources, the program evolved with community input to include other disciplines in agriculture, such as economics, range science, and wildlife and fisheries, and disciplines in family and consumer sciences, such as nutrition, food science, human development, family studies and early childhood education. The inclusion of these disciplines represents a direct response to critical needs in South Dakota Indian communities such as land management, diabetes prevention, economic development and individual, family and community well-being.

People

Ethnicity mattered in the selection and empowerment of 2+2+2 participants. As one participant said, "The people made all the difference." Many researchers (Gray 1985; Selsky 1991; Sharfman and Gray 1991) concur, suggesting that any successful collaborative endeavor requires conveners, activists and boundary spanners—those who can relate to multiple groups and mediate differences.

In the 2+2+2, Native American faculty and staff at SDSU were immediately consulted and integrated into program offerings. For example, the university's Native American adviser attended campus visit programs and discussed the resources her office provides Native students on campus. An American Indian faculty member from the journalism department helped organize workshops on newswriting and photography for students. Indian faculty from the tribal colleges and reservation high schools were also important players on the project team, helping to plan, organize and recruit for events, and serving as local links for program participants. Effort was also made to stay in touch with students' families and home communities via personal correspondence, newsletters, and press releases on project activities for the state's American Indian media.

Fredrik Barth (1969) suggests that ethnic identity is constructed through perceptions and interactions, that is, how you see yourself and how others see you. With 2+2+2, effort was made to ensure that these interactions were positive and that affirming messages were sent. Current Native American SDSU students assisted younger 2+2+2 students by showing them around campus, serving as counselors, facilitating workshops and sharing their own stories of challenge and success. In addition, tribal community leaders were involved as keynote speakers. By involving Native people in the development and implementation of the project, student participants were able to see role models of other Indians who were successful academically and professionally, who believed in the 2+2+2 program, and who saw SDSU as a trusted partner. In this way, the educational ladder proposed by the project became more realistic for Native American youth.

Respecting and Responding

The unique needs of American Indian students were taken into account throughout implementation of the 2+2+2. Examples have included providing free child care to students with young children as well as tuition waivers at the SDSU preschool. This proved particularly important in working with tribal college transfer students, whose average age is approximately 30 and who are often single parents. Indeed, all of the first four students to graduate from the 2+2+2 enrolled their children in the preschool. Free tutoring assistance was provided for all Native American students at SDSU, and an emergency fund was available. Assistance with particular needs, such as dealing with the Indian Health Service and securing family housing, was also provided. Culturally sensitive support systems (such as intervention with instructors during student absences caused by death or other family crises) also have been established.

Responding to American Indian student needs in respectful ways was also apparent in the development of curriculum and instruction. For example, when faculty explored collaboration in wildlife and animal/range sciences, the special relationship between the Lakota people and the bison surfaced. While traditionally trained university scientists saw bison as "a bovine species with a hump and an extra rib," American Indians saw them as the sacred "buffalo nation." Likewise, nutrition experts explored issues of diabetes prevention on the reservation, respectful of contexts including lack of money, quality of commodity foods and incorporation of physical activities that were part of the Lakota people's traditional lifestyle. Other examples included exploration of the Lakota extended family concept (*tiospaye*) in family studies courses and the study of American Indian elders in gerontology classes.

Putting Culture Up Front

Several researchers have found strong ethnic identity to be linked to enhanced self-esteem and academic performance (Gay 1994; Martinez and Dukes 1997; Phinney, Cantu, and Kurtz 1997). Many of the strategies discussed above describe how ethnicity matters or is woven into the *background* of the 2+2+2 program tapestry. In several instances, however, culture and ethnicity were featured *up front* in program planning and implementation. In these ways, the program actively promoted the development of a strong American Indian ethnic identity among student participants.

For example, virtually all 2+2+2 gatherings began and were concluded with traditional Lakota prayers. Student recreational activities included learning Native American hand games. Featured food at project events was Indian frybread, soups made from dried corn and buffalo meat, and teas brewed from Native plants. Student sessions were modeled after "talking circles," a traditional American Indian means of discussion. Tribal elders from students' home reservations were invited to share stories and crafts. Students worked together to construct a 2+2+2 quilt, adopting a Lakota star logo. On multiple occasions, students reflected on the relevance of the medicine wheel values of bravery, fortitude, generosity and wisdom to their lives. Students often "smudged" with smoke from burning sage at the beginning of important events to ask for the creator's guidance and to acknowledge the significance of the activity to be undertaken. Special 2+2+2 sweat lodge ceremonies were also held for Native American students in conjunction with important project events and milestones.

Barriers to Success

This chapter began by reviewing the status of American Indian higher education and by explaining how the 2+2+2 program, with its six key components, was successfully launched to address a critical need. Next how ethnicity matters in 2+2+2 was discussed in some detail.

The following two sections will take a different tack. The first section will cover some of the *barriers to success* that 2+2+2 organizers faced, and the second section will highlight some of the *catalysts for change* that helped the program overcome its challenges and achieve its goals.

Lack of Trust Between Partners

Initially, the most significant barrier to project success was a lack of trust between partners in the collaboration. The network of relationships so important for a project such as 2+2+2 simply did not exist. Further compounding this reality was that some tribal colleges recalled instances when SDSU had not followed through with some of its commitments to previous collaborative endeavors, thus weakening the institution's credibility with Native partners. The legacy of displacement, of oppression and of boarding schools (which took Native American children from their homes and families, and which punished tribal youth for speaking their language) compounded this lack of trust. Sue Newell and Jacky Swan (2000) highlight the problems of developing trust when participants hold different worldviews and embrace different value systems. As Adrian Webb (1991) suggests, trust can be the "pivotal microdynamic" of collaboration, and genuine collaboration cannot occur in the presence of suspicion.

In the early years of 2+2+2, much time and effort was spent in developing what Newell and Swan (2000) describe as "companion trust." This involved visiting tribal communities, listening, committing to action and conscientious following through. Several planning retreats were held on reservations and were facilitated by tribal educators. These brought partners together as equals in the program. During these sessions, project goals were crystallized, and strategies were put in motion. After having Native voices heard in the planning process, trust began to grow. Indeed, building relationships amounted to the project's most significant early outcome.

Geographic Distance

Geographic distance was also a barrier to project success. This is in keeping with the findings of Barbara Gray (1985) and Meg Bond and Christopher Keys (1993). Forming strong collaborative relationships with busy people hundreds of miles away proved challenging. Although project staff often visited tribal colleges and reservation high schools, distance and time made it difficult to increase the number of university staff who made regular appearances in Indian communities. Similarly, visiting the SDSU campus for tribal students and schools with limited financial resources (and oftentimes unreliable transportation) was a challenge. Despite these barriers, resources were secured to support regular travel by SDSU staff to participating tribal high schools and colleges. In addition, SDSU visit programs for tribal students and staff were sponsored on numerous occasions throughout the year. Regular letters, frequent e-mails, a project Web site and a 2+2+2 newsletter were other important tools for keeping partners connected across the miles.

Cultural Distance

Culturally, SDSU is a very different place than any of the participating tribal high schools or colleges. SDSU is a university of more than 10,500 students with approximately 150 Native American students. SDSU is located in a conservative, Midwestern farming community. This stands in stark contrast to the state's Indian reservations, tribal high schools and tribal colleges (the largest of which enrolls approximately 1,000 students); all of these are predominantly American Indian. To bridge these cultural distances, efforts were made to make SDSU a more welcoming place for Native American students. Support from numerous campus entities enhanced the university's Native American literature and art collections and sponsored Native American speakers and entertainers. Faculty development efforts were aimed at topics such as Native American learning styles. SDSU also sought to strengthen the academic advising of Native American students and to incorporate more American Indian perspectives into courses across the curriculum.

Lack of Funding

Lack of funding was also an initial barrier to success. A comprehensive intervention such as 2+2+2 is expensive. Tribal colleges, reservation high schools and prospective American Indian student participants needed financial incentives to participate. Federal grants, when acquired, were distributed equitably among project partners. These funds went a long way toward ameliorating need. Still, with much of the financial support for 2+2+2 coming from external grants, various aspects of the program (such as scholarships and distance education) have had more or less activity over time depending on varying funding levels. Further, continually seeking grant resources sometimes took staff time and energy away from larger programmatic considerations. As the program has matured, more responsibility for ongoing financial support has been absorbed by the project partners.

Lack of Previous Success

Initially, systems simply were not in place to facilitate student success across educational levels in the 2+2+2. While programs existed to support students at the high school, the tribal college and the university level, the "glue" or connecting mechanisms were missing.

When the 2+2+2 was new, no program completers could vouch for it. One initial challenge for 2+2+2 was to create its own success stories. Gradually, these began to emerge—in signed agreements, revised courses, successful experiential learning programs and eventually in program graduates. Small successes and project milestones were publicized and celebrated.

Catalysts for Change

These successes resulted from several key catalysts for change, which either existed at the partner institutions or which were acquired when needed by the collaborative efforts of the partners. These catalysts for change will be discussed next.

Committed People

One of the catalysts for change were the many people at all levels of the project who were committed to working for the good of Native American students. Early planning retreats brought these talented, passionate professionals together with a common purpose. Others who wanted to be involved in outreach programming to Native American communities now had a mechanism to do so. Supportive administrators at SDSU and at other partner institutions removed structural barriers and provided the moral and financial support for the program to get under way.

Outside Funding

Securing outside funding provided resources for more people to get involved. This also raised the project's profile among the SDSU campus community. An aggressive, collaborative team of grant writers, composed of faculty and staff at all three educational levels (reservation high schools, tribal colleges and SDSU) worked together successfully to pull in funding from sources such as the U.S. Department of Agriculture's Higher Education Challenge Grants and Multicultural Scholars programs, the U.S. Department of Education's Fund for the Improvement of Post-Secondary Education, and the National Institute of Health's Bridges to the Baccalaureate Program.

Fortuitous Timing

Timing for the project was another catalyst for change. SDSU was emphasizing diversity and recruiting more Native American students. Reservation high schools were eager to see more of their students attend college. Tribal colleges were hoping to have a larger share of their students complete associate degrees and eventually baccalaureate degrees. Reservation communities wanted more of their own people serving in professional, leadership capacities.

Philosophical Scaffolding

This chapter so far has provided specific information about the 2+2+2 program—its key components, the challenges faced and the successes achieved. The next section will cover the philosophical scaffolding that supports 2+2+2. The following theoretical concepts will be discussed:

- the construction of self, particularly in a social context that allows students to define themselves as successful;
- the creation of various forms of capital (cultural, bonding and bridging);
- confronting individual and institutionalized discrimination;

- systems change of indifferent and / or hostile educational environments; and
- the empowerment of students to help them succeed academically.

Defining Success

Creating a culture within the 2+2+2 program that defined each American Indian student participant as *successful* was important to overall project *success*. Ann Swidler (1986) explains that students carry with them "cultural tool kits," and the fact that they are filled with unique knowledge, experiences and insights needs to be affirmed and celebrated. Daphna Oyserman, Larry Gant, and Joel Ager (1995) further argue that schools and the interactions students experience there play an important role in minority students' construction of self—helping them answer the questions "Who am I?" and "What might I become?"

The 2+2+2 program affirms students' success from the outset, emphasizing that a strong American Indian ethnic identity is linked to academic achievement and college graduation. Vincent Tinto's seminal work on student attrition (Tinto 1975) suggests that interventions aimed at helping minority students should focus on helping them overcome their deficits. The 2+2+2 program takes a different approach, one aimed at student empowerment. The higher education system itself is examined, and ways to build on students' strengths are sought (Tierney 1992).

The 2+2+2 program tackles this challenge in a number of ways. Following are several examples. Participants were required to complete application forms, write brief essays describing why they wanted to participate and obtain instructors' endorsements before being selected for the 2+2+2 summer institute or research apprentice program. While the selection process was not extremely competitive for summer institute (with more than 80 percent of all applicants chosen to participate), completing the process gave students a sense of accomplishment, along with some experience in filling out college forms. Congratulatory letters were then sent to the students, their families and school sponsors.

"Congratulations" and "welcome" were the predominant themes in the event's first day of activity. This not only made the students feel successful as individuals, but in looking around at their fellow participants, they all were made to feel part of a select group of Native American scholars. The 2+2+2 student photographs were featured on project brochures, a Web site and a traveling display. When viewing these materials, students would often identify siblings, cousins or other older students from their reservations in the featured photographs. This was further testimony for the potential success of Native American students. Other strategies for helping participants see themselves as successful were awards ceremonies, project T-shirts, news releases about student accomplishments and special honoring programs when students graduated.

Creating Capital

American Indian students are sometimes seen as lacking in the "cultural capital" (Bourdieu 1977) needed to succeed in higher education. (The term "cultural capital" has been discussed in some detail in Chapters One and Two.) Cultural capital may include having educated parents and having access to technology (Huffman 1999). Discussions of cultural capital suggest a "deficit-driven model" (Guajardo and Guajardo 2002:286), best illustrated by the question, "What do these students need in order to succeed in higher education?" The 2+2+2 program instead takes an "assets-based approach" (Guajardo and Guajardo 2002:286). The program sends positive messages about what Native American students *do* bring to school in their cultural tool kits (Swidler 1986) and further adds to those tool kits an enhanced knowledge of higher education and a broad network of social support. As an acknowledgment of the strengths they bring, individual 2+2+2 students are invited to share their stories and skills with the larger group.

Robert Putnam (2000) furthered the definition of capital by describing both "bonding" and "bridging" elements of the phenomenon. "Bonding capital" is developed through strong connections within relatively homogeneous groups, such as one's family or one's community. The 2+2+2 program builds students' bonding capital by creating linkages with teachers and peers in home schools and communities.

"Bridging capital" (Putnam 2000) refers to the students' broader social network. One of the significant outcomes of 2+2+2 has been to help students form bridges from high school to tribal college, from tribal college to SDSU, and from home school peers to other student participants. High school teachers, community leaders, college students and university staff all become part of the 2+2+2 participants' social network. This network of student friends and resource persons helps 2+2+2 students succeed academically.

Confronting Discrimination

William Tierney (1992), who conducted interviews with Native American students in several colleges and universities, concludes that most higher education institutions are indifferent, rather than hostile, to minorities. Overt acts of racism may not readily be apparent but, according to Tierney (1992), a lack of understanding of minority issues is a constant theme on many college campuses. Officially, Native American students are encouraged, but too often institutionally they find discouragement (Tierney 1992).

Sociologists distinguish between "individual discrimination," which is overt action on the part of individuals that depreciates minorities, and "institutionalized discrimination," which is the customary way of doing things in society that keeps minorities in a subordinate position (Ferrante 1992:295–296). The 2+2+2 program actively works to counter both kinds of discrimination. Programs sponsored by 2+2+2 to address individual discrimination have included:

- sessions for faculty on confronting racism in the classroom,
- workshops for residential hall advisers, and
- Native American speakers who discuss with campuswide audiences personal experiences with discrimination.

Systems Change

The 2+2+2 project also acknowledges that institutionalized discrimination exists in the form of taken-for-granted policies and practices that limit access to higher education for Native Americans. The project is explicitly aimed at ensuring equal educational access for American Indian students.

The 2+2+2 project has aggressively undertaken "systems change" at SDSU. "Systems change" refers to transformations at the institutional level that have long-term impacts. Some examples include:

- The articulation agreements developed through 2+2+2 are now official documents that govern how credits transfer between institutional partners.
- Curriculum changes, supported through 2+2+2 minigrants, have integrated American Indian perspectives into a wide variety of courses. As a result, the broader campus student body is getting a more diversified education.

• Faculty who have participated in 2+2+2 visits and in special teaching/research/advising workshops have built capacity for more effectively working with Native American students.

• The 2+2+2 summer institute has become an annual, institution-sponsored event.

• Significant college resources are now directed toward scholarships for American Indian students, and new SDSU Foundation scholarships for Native American students have been created.

• Momentum generated through 2+2+2 has helped to spur a broader range of Native American outreach and support activities across campus. This constellation of projects not present when the project began includes TRiO Student Support Services, Upward Bound, a minority recruiter, a Native American nursing program, an Office for Diversity Enhancement, the SDSU-Flandreau Indian School Success Academy (mentioned in Chapter One), a graduate cohort program for tribal college faculty, and numerous collaborative SDSU/tribal college research projects.

Student Empowerment

Tierney (2000:228) points out that successful college preparatory programs for minorities acknowledge that discrimination exists, but work actively to help students figure out ways to overcome discrimination. The 2+2+2 program certainly follows the Tierney model.

To this end, current Native American students and 2+2+2 alumni have shared, during panel discussions with younger students, their personal stories of dealing with racism and discrimination on campus. Key messages in these sessions have included coping strategies, developing a network of support and connecting with campus services like the counseling center and the Native American student advisement office.

To repeat, the 2+2+2 project, rather than trying to change individual students by compensating for their weaknesses, views its mission as changing the entire campus environment so that Native Americans can be successful there. The goal for 2+2+2 students is not to become integrated into the educational system that currently exists, but rather to become capable of altering it (Tierney 1992).

Summary

The 2+2+2 program represents an innovative, collaborative approach to empowering Native American students through completion of their baccalaureate degrees. More than 500 students have attended 2+2+2 workshops. Approximately 50 have earned academic scholarships to pursue college degrees. And, thanks in part to 2+2+2, more than 20 American Indian students have graduated from SDSU and are now working as professionals in reservation communities.

In addition, the program has spurred meaningful development for more than 75 SDSU, tribal college and reservation high school faculty members who have participated in 2+2+2. As a result, these individuals are now better equipped to collaborate for enhanced teaching, outreach and research programs that benefit American Indians in South Dakota and beyond.

Institutional changes at SDSU have occurred both in terms of specific policy (for example, acceptance of tribal college credit) and also in terms of a generally more positive, proactive stance toward partnerships with American Indian educators. A variety of new programs have spun off of the 2+2+2; these have led to far greater institutional involvement with tribal communities.

In each of these cases, ethnicity has not only *mattered* with the 2+2+2, ethnicity has been at the *heart of the matter*. Integral to every aspect of the program's success have been reciprocal sensitivity, learning, inclusion and celebration of the strengths of American Indian culture. Through openness, acknowledgment and support of a strong, positive American Indian ethnic identity, 2+2+2 students have been affirmed in their pursuit of educational and career aspirations.

References

American Indian Higher Education Consortium. 1999. *Tribal Colleges: An Introduction*. Alexandria, Va.: Tribal College Research and Data Base Initiative.

Baer, Linda, Donald Arwood, and Velva-Lu Spencer. 1994. "Reservations: Basis for Development." *South Dakota Farm and Home Research* 39(1):14–16.

Baird, Phil. 1996. *What Is a Tribal Land Grant College?* Rosebud, S.D.: W. K. Kellogg Foundation, Sinte Gleska University.

Barth, Fredrik. 1969. *Ethnic Groups and Boundaries*. London: Allen and Unwin.

Belgarde, W. Larry. 1993. "Indian Control and the Management of Dependencies: The Case of Tribal Community Colleges." Ph.D. dissertation, Stanford University, Palo Alto, Calif.

Bond, Meg A. and Christopher Keys. 1993. "Empowerment, Diversity and Collaboration: Promoting Synergy on Community Boards." *American Journal of Community Psychology* 21:37–57.

Bourdieu, Pierre. 1977. *Outline of a Theory of Practice*. Cambridge: Cambridge University Press.

Boyer, Paul. 1997. *Native American Colleges: Progress and Prospects—A Special Report to the Carnegie Foundation for the Advancement of Teaching*. San Francisco: Jossey-Bass Publishers.

Carter, Carolyn. 1999. *Education and Development in Poor Rural Communities: An Interdisciplinary Research Agenda*. Charleston, W.Va.: ERIC Document Reproduction Service.

Crazy Bull, Cheryl. 1997. "A Native Conversation About Scholarship." *Tribal College* 9(1):17–24.

Feagin, Joe, Vera Hernan, and Nikitah Imani. 1996. *The Agony of Education*. New York: Routledge.

Ferrrante, Joan. 1992. *Sociology: A Global Perspective*. Belmont, Calif.: Wadsworth Publishing Company.

Garrod, Andrew and Colleen Larimore, eds. 1997. *First Person, First Peoples: Native American College Students Tell Their Life Stories*. Ithaca, N.Y.: Cornell University Press.

Gay, Geneva. 1994. "Coming of Age Ethnically: Teaching Young Adolescents of Color." *Theory Into Practice* 33(3):149–155.

Gray, Barbara. 1985. "Conditions Facilitating Interorganizational Collaboration." *Human Relations* 38:911–936.

Guajardo, Miguel A. and Francisco J. Guajardo. 2002. "Critical Ethnography and Community Change." Pp. 281–304 in *Ethnography and Schools: Qualitative Approaches to the Study of Education*, edited by Y. Zou and H. T. Trueba. Lanham, Md.: Rowman & Littlefield Publishers.

Harvey, William B. 2001. *Minorities in Higher Education 2000–2001: 18th Annual Status Report.* Washington, D.C.: American Council on Education.

Huffman, Terry E. 1999. *Cultural Masks: Ethnic Identity and American Indian Higher Education.* Buckhannon, W.Va.: Stone Creek Press.

Kids Count Data Book. 1997. Baltimore: The Annie E. Casey Foundation.

Lal, Barbara Ballis. 1995. "Symbolic Interaction Theories." *American Behavioral Scientist* 3:421–444.

Martinez, Ruben O. and Richard L. Dukes. 1997. "The Effects of Ethnic Identity, Ethnicity and Gender on Adolescent Well-Being." *Journal of Youth & Adolescence* 26(5):503–516.

McDonald, Joseph. 2000. "Building Extension Partnerships to Achieve Better Indian Communities Through 1994 Land Grant Institutions." Presented at the annual meeting of the National Association of State Universities and Land Grant Colleges, November, San Antonio, Texas.

Nagel, Joane. 1994. "Constructing Ethnicity: Creating and Recreating Identity and Culture." *Social Problems* 1:152–176.

Newell, Sue and Jacky Swan. 2000. "Trust and Interorganizational Networking." *Human Relations* 53:1287–1318.

Nichols, Laurie Stenberg and Tim Nichols. 1998. "2+2+2: Collaborating to Enhance Educational Opportunities for Native Americans." *Journal of Family and Consumer Sciences* 90:38–41.

Nichols, Timothy, Phil Baird, and Diane Kayongo-Male. 2001. "Partnerships Offer Promise and Perils: A Study of Collaboration With State Universities." *Tribal College Journal* 13(2):20–23.

Oppelt, Norman T. 1990. *The Tribally Controlled Indian Colleges: The Beginnings of Self Determination in American Indian Education.* Tsaile, Ariz.: Navajo Community College Press.

Oyserman, Daphna, Larry Gant, and Joel Ager. 1995. "A Socially Contextualized Model of African American Identity: Possible Selves and School Persistence." *Journal of Personality and Social Psychology* 69:1216–1232.

Pavel, D. Michael, Rececca Rak Skinner, Elizabeth Farris, Margaret Calahan, John Tippeconnic, and Wayne Stein. 1998. *American Indians and Alaska Natives in Postsecondary Education.* Washington, D.C.: National Center for Education Statistics.

Pertusati, Linda. 1988. "Beyond Segregation or Integration: A Case Study from Effective Native American Education." *Journal of American Indian Education* 27(2):10–20.

Phinney, Jean S., Cindy Lou Cantu, and Dawn A. Kurtz. 1997. "Ethnic and American Identity as Predictors of Self-Esteem Among African American, Latino, and White Adolescents." *Journal of Youth & Adolescence* 26(2):165–185.

Putnam, Robert D. 2000. *Bowling Alone: The Collapse and Revival of American Community.* New York: Simon and Schuster.

Selsky, John W. 1991. "Lessons in Community Development: An Activity Approach to Stimulating Interorganizational Collaboration." *Journal of Applied Behavioral Science* 27:91–115.

Sharfman, Mark and Barbara Gray. 1991. "The Context of Interorganizational Collaboration in the Garment Industry: An Institutional Perspective." *Journal of Applied Behavioral Science* 27:181–208.

Stein, Wayne. 1992. *Tribally Controlled Colleges: Making Good Medicine.* New York: Peter Lang.

St. Germaine, Richard. 1995. *Drop Out Rates among American Indians and Alaska Native Students: Beyond Cultural Discontinuity.* Charleston, W.Va.: Clearinghouse on Rural Education and Small Schools, Appalachia Educational Laboratory.

Swidler, Ann. 1986. "Culture in Action: Symbols and Strategies." *American Sociological Review* 51:273–286.

Szasz, Margaret. 1999. *Education and the American Indian: The Road to Self Determination Since 1928.* Albuquerque: University of New Mexico Press.

Tierney, William G. 1992. *Official Encouragement, Institutional Discouragement: Minorities in Academe—The Native American Experience.* Norwood, N.J.: Ablex.

———. 1993. *Building Communities of Difference: Higher Education in the Twenty-First Century.* Toronto, Ontario: OISE Press.

———. 1998. *The Responsive University: Restructuring for High Performance.* Baltimore: Johns Hopkins University Press.

———. 2000. "Power, Identity and the Dilemma of College Student Departure." Pp. 213–234 in *Rethinking the Student Departure Puzzle,* edited by J. M. Braxton. Nashville: Vanderbilt University Press.

Tinto, Vincent. 1975. "Dropouts from Higher Education: A Theoretical Synthesis of Recent Research." *Review of Educational Research* 45:89–125.

Trueba, Henry T. and Yali Zou. 1994. *Power in Education: The Case of Miao University Students and its Significance for American Culture.* Washington, D.C.: The Falmer Press.

Wax, Murray, Rosalie Wax, and Robert Dumont Jr. 1964. *Formal Education in an American Indian Community: Peer Society and the Failure of Minority Education.* Prospect Heights, Ill.: Waveland Press.

Webb, Adrian. 1991. "Co-ordination: A Problem in Public Sector Management." *Policy and Politics* 19:229–241.

W. K. Kellogg Foundation. 1999. *Returning to our Roots: The Engaged Institution*. Washington, D.C.: National Association of State Universities and Land Grant Colleges.

Wright, Bobby and William G. Tierney. 1991. "American Indians in Higher Education: A History of Cultural Conflict." *Change* 23:11–18.

4

First Generation Student Success Program: Latino/a Students and Families Working Together

Derek Vergara and Len Hightower

The University of La Verne is a small, private school located about 35 miles from downtown Los Angeles. During its first century, from the 1890s to the 1990s, the undergraduate student body at the University of La Verne evolved into one of the most diverse student bodies among all the other small, private colleges in California.

Over half of the University of La Verne's students are minorities—32 percent Latino/a, 12 percent Asian American, 7 percent African American and 1 percent American Indian. Among the one third of La Verne's students who are Latino/a, the percentage who are also first generation college students has ranged from 56 percent to 80 percent since 1985.

First Generation Student Success Program

The First Generation Student Success Program (FGSSP) began in 1996 to address the needs of two important segments of La Verne's population—first generation college students and minority students, the largest percentage of whom are Latino/a. Since then FGSSP has served 450 students.

FGSSP has five program elements, all designed to foster students' academic, professional and personal success. The FGSSP elements are:

- a scholarship program;
- new student and family orientation;
- family engagement services;

- a mentoring program; and
- research.

FGSSP differs significantly from other minority college preparation and retention efforts in that it is "a data-driven program" (Reisberg 1999:A43). The University of La Verne received a three-year, $500,000 grant from the James Irvine Foundation in 1995 to fund two activities. The first was a study, designed to better understand the obstacles faced by first generation college students (especially those who were also minority group members). The second activity funded by the grant was a retention program aimed at helping these students and their families overcome obstacles and obtain degrees. FGSSP is the retention effort that resulted from the initial study.

At the time of FGSSP's inception, some provocative legislative propositions and various private organizations were unapologetically opposed to race-related initiatives within higher education. These proposals challenged institutions of higher education, such as La Verne, to think creatively about their race-related strategies regarding admissions, retention and research to avoid potential lawsuits. The notion of focusing on first generation college students seemed feasible and circumvented the issue of race-related measures, since white students were also identified as part of the first generation college student population.

This chapter will begin by presenting some of the research findings that provided the scaffolding for FGSSP. The research findings will focus on:

- first generation college students as a whole;
- more specifically, on first generation Latino/a students at the University of La Verne; and
- even more specifically, on first generation Latina students at La Verne.

Then the founding of FGSSP itself will be discussed, with an emphasis on the five primary elements that constitute the program. A final section of the chapter will evaluate and summarize FGSSP's successes and challenges to date.

Data That Drive FGSSP

The first step toward the founding of FGSSP was a three-year study, which began in the 1996–1997 academic year. As mentioned earlier, the study was intended to help the University of La Verne, and perhaps other colleges, understand and remove some of the barriers faced by first generation college students, especially those who were also minorities (Reisberg 1999:A43). Some of the findings—about first generation college students and about first generation Latino and Latina students at the University of La Verne—will be presented in the following sections.

First Generation College Students

Although there has been a dramatic increase in research on first generation college students in the past decade, relatively little had been published before the 1990s. First generation college students are defined as those whose parents did not attend college. Their parents' highest level of education is a high school diploma or less (National Center for Education Statistics 1998). Ample literature suggests that first generation college students are more at risk of dropping out than non–first generation college students (Terenzini et al. 1996). According to a report by the U.S. Department of Education's National Center for Education Statistics (1998), first generation college students are more likely to come from families that have lower incomes and that feel being well off financially is important. Higher education may be viewed as a ticket to upward social and financial mobility. First generation college students also tend to enroll part-time, attend two-year public institutions and take remedial courses. Furthermore, these students state that being able to live at home and being able to work while attending school influence their decisions about attending college.

The passage into college for first generation students represents a dramatic break from past family decisions and norms against attending college. Parents of first generation college students have not participated in higher education, which historically has been the foundation for a better quality of life, the catalyst for improving one's socioeconomic status and the ticket for acceptance into mainstream America (Terenzini et al. 1993).

For many first generation college students, going to the university is synonymous with breaching traditional family codes of unity and loyalty. These students often enter college with some level of social distance between themselves and their families (Prieto-Bayard 1999). The cognitive and affective development that occurs as a result of attending college (Pascarella and Terenzini 1991) comes at the expense of family relationships for many first generation college students. The trade-offs can be traumatizing as students sacrifice their close ties with family members in order to succeed in school. While going on to higher education is regarded as a natural rite of passage for students whose parents have attended college, the experience of many first generation college students is disillusioning, filled with abnormalities that are far from being natural.

The journey into college is often filled with many challenges and disappointments for first generation college students. Expectations for an easy transition from high school to college are frequently crushed as these students encounter isolation and alienation. First generation college students must expend additional time and energy trying to understand a perplexing higher education system, with norms foreign to them but understood by the rest of the campus community.

When disaggregating the data by ethnicity and gender, first generation college students were found less likely to be white and male and more likely to be Latino/a and female. Research conducted on first generation college students at the University of La Verne revealed that they were quite similar to first generation college students studied nationally (Prieto-Bayard 1999).

First Generation Latino and Latina Students at the University of La Verne

Research conducted by the University of La Verne's Office of Institutional Research indicates that a high number of entering students are the first in their families to go to college. Many of these first generation college students come from ethnically diverse backgrounds, with the majority being Latino/a. As mentioned earlier, since 1985 the percentage of entering Latino/a students who are first in their families to attend college has ranged from 56 percent to 80 percent.

These students come from both rural and urban backgrounds. The increase in first generation Latino/a students, however, is mainly due to the university's primary recruitment area, which is roughly the greater Los Angeles region. A high percentage of students who enter La Verne come from cities that are 50 miles or less from the university, all of which have large Latino/a communities.

Seeing that these students receive a quality education and a positive academic experience is in the hands of administrators, faculty and staff at the University of La Verne. There was initial resistance to conduct race-related studies from some, but many more seemed eager to learn about Latino/a students.

One important lesson learned was that Latino/a students often experience cultural and family pressures that interfere with decisions about going to college and with the ability to be successful while in college. Moreover, family pressure can be so great that a decision to attend a college near home seems more feasible than a decision to attend a college out of state. For most Latino/a students, the local community college is the nearest school to home.

Laura Rendon and Manuel Justiz (1989) have studied precollege, culturally based indicators that affect the transition of Latino/a students into college. These same factors often affect the students' entire tenure in college (Rendon and Justiz 1989). Many of the factors studied by Rendon and Justiz are present in the Latino/a student population at the University of La Verne. Latino/a students frequently come from groups with low socioeconomic status. Consequently, students are expected to work, sometimes two jobs, during college to contribute to the family income. College attendance for Latino/a students sometimes involves moving away from friends and family, experiencing self-doubt and being perceived as different. For students whose families speak Spanish at home, using English at school can be difficult and confusing. The ability to deal with familial pressures and to balance conflicting roles is a strong indicator of college success.

Mary Prieto-Bayard, a psychology professor at the University of La Verne, has examined the social distance between first generation students and their families during the critical freshman year of college (Prieto-Bayard 1999). Her respondents included many first generation Latino/a college students. These students experienced varying degrees of social distance from their families, classified into four categories:

• *Authority and control.* Past authoritative landscapes are being challenged and are shifting, resulting in frustration and in perceived defiance by the student and the institution. For example, one father could not comprehend why he did not have access to his child's grades, while another father continued to uphold curfew rules when his daughter was at home visiting.

• *Lack of understanding by parents of college demands and the necessity for students to explain attendance at campus activities.* The disconnect occurs when students try to justify the importance of their school agendas and of the new roles they have attained. For example, a student who had just become the president of his fraternity relates his mother's reaction: "Oh, president of a fraternity, *mijo*, how wonderful! I am so proud of you! A fraternity *mijo*! What is a fraternity?"

While the mother is able to give ample emotional support to her son's interests, she has trouble translating that support into "tangible, instrumental behaviors" (Prieto-Bayard 1997). This, in turn, leaves the son feeling deprived when sharing his experiences.

• *Shift in values.* The increased knowledge and new experiences gained in college often result in changes in the personal philosophies of students after they enter the university. Their perspective is no longer as concrete, but rather has multiple dimensions. This shift often brings students into direct conflict with family, friends and cultural beliefs. There is a constant struggle to live in two worlds, the world that defines the students within their heritage and the world of academia (Rendon 1994; Terenzini et al. 1994). The fear of not fitting into either world has negative implications, resulting in alienation, self-doubt and psychological distress (Rendon 1992; London 1989).

• *Family expectations.* Students carry into college with them pre-existing roles, established by family traditions. As the pressures of college conflict with the expectations of family, the resulting dichotomy can be daunting, leaving students feeling confused and misguided. Although the pressure of family expectations are felt generally by both first generation Latino and Latina students, more pressure is felt by Latinas.

Special Concerns of First Generation Latina Students at the University of La Verne

Family expectations influence many of the decisions that Latinas make about college (Rendon and Valdez 1993). Rendon and Justiz (1989) have found that Latino/a parents with a limited knowledge of higher education frequently advise their daughters to pursue degrees that prove to be restrictive in the job market. Although significant change is occurring, in many Latino/a families traditional norms about women and their roles as caretakers still hold sway. Daughters who live in residence halls and enroll full time may not be available to watch younger siblings and assume household responsibilities while parents are working. Such conflicts are examples of the ongoing struggle between college and family expectations (Rendon and Justiz 1989). Ultimately, the Latinas' choices to socially and academically engage in college full time may be viewed as dishonoring traditional roles as nurturers within the family structure (Rendon and Justiz 1989).

In a study of La Verne's first generation Latina students, Prieto-Bayard (1999) found that Latino/a parents who had not attended college did not understand why their daughters had to be at school on days when they had no classes. These parents also could not understand why their daughters did not attend family functions on weekends or why their daughters had to study when they were at home visiting. The following comment, from a first generation Latina student, serves as an example: "My parents just don't understand my life now. I have changed in just about every way imagined, and I realize that when I go home or when my family comes to visit me. How am I supposed to act? Who am I supposed to be for these people? I think differently, I am more open."

As part of the same study, Prieto-Bayard (1999) examined how Latinas regarded their status in relation to other students and faculty. Surprisingly, over half expressed feeling no different than other students. Overall they reported feeling an atmosphere of acceptance and a welcoming environment. A sizable number of respondents, however, felt they were less favorably perceived regarding academic capability. Many Latinas felt the need to break down stereotypes of Latinas. This dynamic resulted in some cultural and identity confusion. As one Latina student states: "It's hard getting used to people looking down on you because they think I'm a *Chola*, just because I'm Latina. I guess that is something I have to get used to." These findings suggest that Latinas at La Verne feel capable and confident about their place in the campus community. They continue, however, to expend extra energy trying to prove themselves as reputable students to those still operating from negative stereotypes about Latinas.

FGSSP: Creating a Retention Program for Students *and* Families

Events Leading to the Establishment of FGSSP

The number of minority students attending the University of La Verne had increased significantly between the mid-1970s and the mid-1990s. (Survey data showed, however, that there was no statistically significant increase in the number of first generation college students enrolled at the University of La Verne during this same time frame.)

With the increase in cultural diversity, there was a greater concern from the administration about racially related incidents among students. Such incidents became more pronounced in the late 1980s and early 1990s. A couple of incidents, which received widespread publicity, were the impetus for action by the Student Affairs Division and the university's senior management. Some specific steps were taken to address minority student concerns and to promote cross-cultural communication, but these steps did not constitute the kind of comprehensive plan that was needed to properly address complex diversity issues.

In 1991 University of La Verne President Stephen C. Morgan formed a campuswide task force to address diversity issues. The task force brought together those who were empathetic to the needs of ethnic minority students and those who were in positions of authority at La Verne. The inclusion of the latter group was important. Individuals in leadership positions could not only see that the needs of minority students were met, but could also institutionalize all the efforts within the fabric of the campus community. All academic deans, student affairs deans, the academic vice president and the president were placed on the task force. Minority students, faculty and staff, as well as other faculty who had special expertise in the area of diversity, were also invited to join the task force. The diversity of the task force itself proved to be fundamental in generating the synergy necessary to accomplish the group's mission.

A study of student satisfaction at the University of La Verne was conducted (covering the years between 1990 and 1995), and a question was asked about racial harmony on campus. The results, when disaggregated by ethnicity, indicated that African American, Asian American and international students continued to rate services, programs and faculty / staff lower than did other student groups.

Demographics of Students and Families
To Be Served by FGSSP

Data on first generation and minority students at the University of La Verne have already been presented. Additional data collected through the University of California, Los Angeles, Cooperative Institutional Research Program (CIRP) confirmed that many of the first generation college students at the University of La Verne were ethnic minorities who also came from lower income families. As reported in the annual CIRP data from 1992 through 1994, the average median household income of minority students at La Verne was $42,895. The average median income of first generation minority students was $27,833. Ninety percent of the first generation minority students at La Verne reported that they had some concerns about financing college.

In general, minority students entered La Verne with Scholastic

Aptitude Test (SAT) scores and high school grade point averages (GPA) lower than white students. African American students scored 397 in math and 381 in verbal, on average, between 1990 and 1994, with GPAs ranging around 2.74. Latino/a students entered with higher SAT scores, 421 in math and 389 in verbal, with GPAs averaging 2.94. This compared well with the school's average entering GPA of 2.98 and with the average white students' entering GPA of 3.03.

According to the results of the CIRP survey at La Verne, ethnic minority students, especially first generation minority students, rated themselves lower than white students when asked about the confidence they felt in their academic abilities. Generally speaking, ethnic minorities who are first in their families to attend college are more likely than other minorities or whites to rate themselves average or below average in overall academic ability, math ability, writing ability and intellectual self-confidence. First generation ethnic minorities also are more likely to believe that they will fail one or more courses, that they will need tutoring, that they will seek counseling, and that they will take remedial English or math courses.

The Creation of FGSSP and Its Five Elements

The events that preceded the start of FGSSP included a number of racially related incidents on campus, negative responses by minorities on a student satisfaction survey and the formation of a task force to address diversity concerns. These events, as well as the changing demographics of the University of La Verne student body, led to the creation of FGSSP. From the beginning, FGSSP's goal has been to help first generation college students persist in college to graduation. In the eyes of FGSSP's creators, academic success for first generation students is strongly tied to family support. Thus, FGSSP sees its role as strengthening students *and* their families as they move together through the college experience.

FGSSP has five program elements, and each will be explained in detail below.

Scholarship program. Nominal scholarships ($500 per semester) are given to about 55 first generation college students during their first two years at La Verne. Recipients must continue to meet the program criteria, which are maintaining good academic standing and being enrolled full time. The scholarships cover the cost of books, supplies, fees, transportation, room and board. The program director is the custodian of the money, which is advantageous in two ways: It ensures active program participation from students, and it allows for spontaneous advising and counseling. The students are required to visit the office to fill out the paperwork necessary to pick up their checks. This allows the staff to engage with the students and give the necessary support on an ongoing basis.

Qualified program participants are identified by information provided by the Office of Undergraduate Admissions. Admissions counselors use the program (and its promise of scholarship money) as part of the recruitment strategy to bring prospective students to La Verne.

New student and family orientation. New student and family orientation originally had three components:

- a summer assessment workshop;
- other workshops to provide motivation and academic self-confidence; and
- initial academic advising, including an introduction to FGSSP and to the university.

Program organizers designed these three activities with several goals in mind. First generation college students and their families needed more knowledge of the admissions and financial aid processes. They also needed to be able to connect with appropriate staff who could answer their questions about college. Furthermore, first generation students and their parents required a forum where they could bring their concerns about college and the challenges college would bring into their lives. FGSSP organizers hoped that during new student and family orientation sessions they could discuss with attendees what they wanted to get out of college and what it would take to fulfill those aspirations.

Many of the goals were met through the summer assessment workshop. Eventually this workshop became embedded in a university-wide new student orientation and was modified to fit into the larger program.

Since having a strong connection to the university is critical for both students and their families, all participants receive La Verne memorabilia—educational supplies, license plates and clothing items embossed with the school logo. Hotel accommodations are arranged for families who travel more than three hours from home. These families also receive stipends for meals and mileage.

Focus groups are conducted concurrently with both students and parents, as a part of an overall strategy to gather empirical evidence to improve program objectives. Due to the large number of Latino/a families involved, appropriate accommodations are made for Spanish-speaking parents. Requests have been received for Vietnamese and Armenian interpreters. Faculty and staff fluent in these languages willingly assist with interpretation. Many of the interpreters were once first generation college student themselves.

Family engagement services. Family members can have a tremendous impact on the academic success of first generation college students. Better communication with students' families throughout the college experience is another goal of FGSSP.

The family engagement services program develops culturally and linguistically appropriate materials to effectively communicate information to families about admissions, registration and the entire college experience. FGSSP tells prospective students and their families what to expect from college and explains to them how to choose majors and careers.

As an example of ongoing engagement with families, the university invites parents to a fall financial aid workshop. The workshop prepares students and families to complete the Free Application for Federal Student Aid (FAFSA) for the coming academic year. The Office of Financial Aid has several Spanish-speaking counselors who attend the workshop and assist with translation. Although the Spanish translating service is fairly common in these situations, the uniqueness that transpires within this particular workshop is in its "spirit of *familia*." The parents convey a sense of trust to workshop presenters, for genuinely caring about their children, and more importantly, for the respect they themselves receive. Parents also are given La Verne memorabilia as a gesture of the university's appreciation for attending the workshop. Parents also receive a personal financial aid contact, should they need more assistance in the FAFSA process.

After one financial aid workshop, a student stated: "What did you say to my dad? He said how proud he was of me and gave me $50. I didn't want to take it because I know $50 is a lot for us. He really wanted me to have it! I didn't know what to say! I'm going to buy the calculator that I need for class."

Mentoring program. Mentoring is provided for each first generation minority student. Mentors are volunteers who come from a variety of groups such as alumni, faculty, staff and junior/senior minority students. Mentors are trained through an initial orientation session and are continually supported in their efforts by the program director.

Students consistently meet with their mentors. They develop a "growth plan" over time, identifying a major, assessing career interests and figuring out strategies for dealing with the challenges of being a first generation college student. Through the mentoring program students learn about the university resources available to them.

Mentors, students and their families gather periodically for various activities, like "getting to know you" dinners. At the end of each year, FGSSP hosts a celebration for students, relatives, mentors and other La Verne faculty and staff. During the ceremony, special awards are given—to students who make the academic dean's honor list, to a mentor who has contributed to the program over and beyond the call of duty, and to parents who have volunteered their time to assist with FGSSP.

Research. Both quantitative and qualitative research methodologies were employed to ensure that rich data were collected to better understand first generation college students at the University of La Verne. The quantitative research was conducted by the university's Office of Institutional Research, while the qualitative research was conducted by the faculty research coordinator for the grant.

Research conducted for FGSSP included:

- a continuing search of the national literature on first generation college students as it related to retention and graduation rates;
- statistical analyses of data on first generation college students, gathered from University of La Verne records and from the CIRP freshman survey;
- a study of the families of FGSSP participants to determine factors germane to first generation college students' decision-making processes;
- a campus climate survey on sensitivity to the needs of the university's ethnically diverse population; and
- a continuous improvement assessment of FGSSP and its five elements (Maack 1998). The results of this continuous improvement assessment will be discussed in more detail in the next section.

Program Evaluation for Continuous Improvement

Frequent program evaluations were conducted to ensure that FGSSP was meeting expected goals and improving services to student participants. At the end of the 2001–2002 academic year, the research team at the Institute for Multicultural Research and Campus Diversity conducted a continuous improvement assessment.

Twenty-three of 32 FGSSP participants were surveyed in semi-structured interviews. The majority of the students were Latino/a (57 percent), female (78 percent) and in their freshman or sophomore year of college (91 percent). Sixty-five percent of participants lived on campus. The remaining 35 percent lived with parents or other relatives. Almost 80 percent of participants were employed and worked between eight and 40 hours per week.

The researchers gathered information regarding study habits and academics generally. On average, participants were enrolled in 15 units of coursework. Interestingly, Latino/a students were enrolled in fewer units on average than first generation students of other ethnic backgrounds. Furthermore, men spent six fewer hours on average studying per week than women. Home and work factors also influenced study habits. Students who lived at home studied an average of five hours less per week than students who lived on campus, whereas students with jobs studied an average of nine hours less per week than their unemployed counterparts.

Participants espoused a variety of reasons for remaining in school. Many students remained in school in order to be self-fulfilled or to ensure their futures. Almost half indicated that they stayed in college to meet their career goals. Common career goals were to obtain a particular job or to be paid well. Family emerged as a primary motivator for many students. Recognizing the sacrifices made on their behalf, students expressed a desire to fulfill the expectations of their families.

Not surprisingly, families were also important sources of support, especially for freshmen. All participants reported that their families were "supportive" or "very supportive" of their academic endeavors. The most common types of support described by students were emotional and financial.

Academic advisers were another important source of support for many students. Sixty-one percent of the students indicated that they were "satisfied" or "very satisfied" with their academic advisers. Students who were satisfied commented that their advisers were accessible and knowledgeable about courses and degree requirements. In contrast, many students were disappointed by advisement. Common complaints were that advisers were unavailable or difficult to reach. Many students reported changing advisers due to these experiences.

Overall, students interviewed were pleased with their interactions with professors. Seventy-eight percent said they were "satisfied" or "very satisfied"; however, only 61 percent felt comfortable speaking with their professors about various issues.

In addition, certain university support services, such as computer labs and the library, were widely used by first generation students. Similarly, 65 percent of participants "sometimes" or "often" participated in study groups. More than half were members of campus organizations. Other services, however, such as the Career Center, the Learning Enrichment Center and the Counseling Center, were underutilized. Almost 50 percent of participants were unaware that La Verne offered nonacademic counseling services.

A desire for greater social support was reflected in students' ideas for improvement of FGSSP. Many students suggested incorporating study groups into the program, and others expressed a desire for increased involvement in the program. Several participants called for greater interaction among FGSSP students, whereas others requested more mentoring. Eighty-six percent of students who attended program workshops found them "helpful" or "very helpful."

Overall, students were satisfied with their involvement in FGSSP. The research, however, did reveal several areas in which improvement was needed. For example, finances continue to be a significant stressor for first generation college students. Although the program provides small scholarships to help cover educational expenses during the first and second years at La Verne, the need for financial support in subsequent years remains strong.

Workshop attendance was negatively affected by time constraints, scheduling conflicts and communication problems. Forty-four percent of the students interviewed did not attend any workshops, and 96 percent missed at least one workshop. Scheduling conflicts were the most common reason for missing workshops. Consequently, it was recommended that reminder calls be made to residence hall rooms for students living on campus and that notifications be sent to the home addresses of students living off campus.

The FGSSP evaluation was generally positive; however, the program needs some fine tuning, primarily in the area of event attendance. Also suggested is broadening FGSSP's scope to serve the entire university's population of first generation college students, not just those currently participating in the program.

Summary

The FGSSP was the catalyst to improve access and retention strategies for first generation college students. The success of the program was measured by the premise that first generation college students at the University of La Verne would persist toward graduation if the proper institutional support mechanisms were in place. Overall, the results of FGSSP were positive for the program's first cohort.

According to a report by Stephen Maack (1999), the retention rate for the first cohort of FGSSP students (those who began school in the fall of 1996) was 86 percent, compared with a retention rate of 76 percent for all other freshmen entering that year. During the next academic year, the retention rate for the Fall 1996 FGSSP cohort was 74 percent, compared with a retention rate of 71 percent for all other new freshmen. During the third academic year, 67 percent of the FGSSP cohort stayed at the University of La Verne, compared with 61 percent of all other freshmen who had entered the institution at the same time. Although one can argue that there were only slight differences in retention rates, the figures do suggest that FGSSP had an important impact on retention for the first group of students served (Maack 1999). The study showed that La Verne was doing an excellent job helping first generation students pursue college degrees.

Factors that attracted the students and their families to La Verne were the small size of the campus, the personal attention from faculty and the proximity to home. These same factors convinced students to stay at La Verne. Consequently, there was a good fit between the ecology of La Verne and parental perceptions of their students' needs (Prieto-Bayard 1999).

Research by Prieto-Bayard (1999) also indicated that the University of La Verne was serving its Latino/a students well. A problem area for Latino/a students was the parents who expected them to conform to house rules when at home and to not enjoy too many new freedoms when at school. These students were frustrated by experiencing new levels of independence at school, only to be expected to return to previous levels of dependence at home.

Balancing the demands of family and school was particularly challenging for Latinas, because their gender roles were generally more traditional. Latinas reported that they were still expected to help with chores, attend family gatherings and socially interact (not study) when home on weekends. Some would neglect their schoolwork when home and then try to catch up when back at college. Others would resist family pressures, which resulted in conflicts with parents and feelings of guilt.

Despite adversity, after completing the first three years of the program, both Latinos and Latinas were found to be persisting, to be engaging in the university community and to be fulfilling their academic aspirations.

The First Generation Student Success Program initially was funded by a three-year, $500,000 grant awarded to the University of La Verne by the James Irvine Foundation in 1995. In 1998 an endowment from the Packard Foundation to the University of La Verne allowed the university to continue granting FGSSP scholarships. An allocation of $100,000 per year by the university president from the general budget now supports FGSSP services. Consequently, FGSSP continues to operate today, increasing college access and retention for Latino/as and other underrepresented students.

References

London, Howard B. 1989. "Breaking Away: A Study of First Generation College Students and Their Families." *American Journal of Education* 97:144–170.

Maack, Stephen C. 1998. "Ethnicity, Class, Generation in College, and Family Involvement: What Makes a Difference in Student Success?" Presented at the annual forum of the Association for Institutional Research, May 19, Minneapolis, Minn.

———. 1999. University of La Verne Memorandum, Retention and GPAs of First Generation Student Success Program Students.

National Center for Education Statistics. 1998. *First-Generation Students: Undergraduates Whose Parents Never Enrolled in Postsecondary Education*. Washington, D.C.: U.S. Department of Education.

Pascarella, Ernest T. and Patrick T. Terenzini. 1991. *How College Affects Students*. San Francisco: Jossey-Bass Publishers.

Prieto-Bayard, Mary. 1997. "Families of First Generation College Students: How College-Ready Are They?" Presented at the annual conference of the California Association for Institutional Research, November 20, San Francisco, Calif.

———. 1999. "First Generation Students and Their Families: Crossing the Social Distance." Presented at the National Conference on Race and Ethnicity in Higher Education, June 4, Memphis, Tenn.

Reisberg, Leo. 1999. "To Help Latino Students, a College Looks to Parents." *The Chronicle of Higher Education,* January 15, pp. A43–A44.

Rendon, Laura I. 1992. "From the Barrio to the Academy: Revelations of a Mexican American Scholarship Girl." Pp. 55–64 in *First Generation Students: Confronting the Cultural Issues* (New Directions for Community Colleges, No. 80), edited by L. S. Zwerling and H. London. San Francisco: Jossey-Bass Publishers.

———. 1994. "Validating Culturally Diverse Students: Toward a New Model of Learning and Student Development." *Innovative Higher Education* 19(1):23–32.

Rendon, Laura I. and Manuel J. Justiz. 1989. *Transfer Education in Southwest Border Community Colleges*. Columbia, S.C.: University of South Carolina Press.

Rendon, Laura I. and Manuel J. Valdez. 1993. "Qualitative Indicators of Hispanic Student Transfer." *Community College Review* 20:4.

Terenzini, Patrick T., Laura I. Rendon, M. Lee Upcraft, Susan B. Millar, Kevin W. Allison, Patricia Gregg, and Romero Jalomo. 1993. *The*

Transition to College: Easing the Passage. University Park, Pa.: National Center on Postsecondary Teaching, Learning, and Assessment.

———. 1994. "The Transition to College: Diverse Students, Diverse Stories." *Research in Higher Education* 35(1):57–73.

Terenzini, Patrick T., Leonard Springer, Patricia M. Yaeger, Ernest T. Pascarella, and Amaury Nora. 1996. "First Generation College Students: Characteristics, Experiences, and Cognitive Development." *Research in Higher Education* 37(1):1–22.

5

Critical Moments: Using College Students' Border Narratives as Sites for Cultural Dialogue

Diane Gillespie, Gillies Malnarich and George Woods

"I tend to have a whole lot of classes where I'm either the only black or one of a couple of blacks—I hate it."

—an African American student, 1993

Educators working in colleges and universities rarely hear students express their feelings so directly. The above quotation does not represent the experience of just one young African American man, nor does the following comment of his female, Hmong peer:

I feel kind of embarrassed (when) I'm...put out in front of the class for a kind of display. I feel kind of belittled because I know I can't do anything about it...and then (there's) the fear of having to go back to the class and face them again the next day.

Many students of color in higher education today do not feel any less marginalized or isolated than these students interviewed more than a decade ago.

At the time these students were interviewed, both were enrolled in an established multicultural program nationally recognized for its efforts to ensure that underrepresented students not only had access to higher education but also completed their degrees. The students spoke freely about their experiences in this program and in other university classes during qualitative research studies conducted by faculty who taught in the program (Seaberry 1994; Valades 1994). If students felt so disconnected and undermined when they attended university classes outside their multicultural learning community, how would other underrepresented students fare on predominantly white campuses without the benefit of a supportive multicultural program? With the exception of tribal colleges and historically black colleges and universities, most institutions of higher education still expect underrepresented students to adapt to traditional academic culture, even if it necessitates leaving one's cultural identity and history outside the classroom door.

In interviews, many underrepresented students have continued to portray how cultural difference marginalizes and isolates them. They come to feel out of place, disconnected or misunderstood and even question whether they belong in college. Such times of trouble stand out for them as *critical moments* in their undergraduate education—times when they consider dropping out because their difference makes them feel unworthy in a predominantly white institution. Such students' stories became the basis for a critical pedagogical intervention called The Critical Moments Project.

This chapter describes The Critical Moments Project from its origins in the Goodrich Scholarship Program at the University of Nebraska at Omaha to its evolution as a campus equity and engagement initiative in Washington State. Drawing on students' accounts of personal experiences in higher education, Critical Moments identifies those patterns of inequity, often buried in the details of ordinary campus life, that need to be uncovered and challenged if students of color, in particular, are to feel at home in higher education. Students are interviewed; their experiences are written as case stories; these stories, in turn, become starting points for discussions in classrooms and other campus settings. The student comments quoted above, for example, became the raw material for well-known Critical Moments case stories, "Survival Soliloquy" and "Being Heard across the Table" (Gillespie and Woods 2000). (For other Critical Moments cases with commentaries, see Gillespie, Seaberry, and Valades 1997; Hansen and Gillespie 1998; Henning and Gillespie 1996; Malnarich and Gillespie 2004; Seaberry and Gillespie 1997; Valades 1996).

The Critical Moments Project weaves together successful educational practices—problem-posing education, case teaching methodology, conceptual frameworks from ethnic studies, and learning in the context of diverse communities. The project privileges underrepresented students' voices: first, to make public their experiences in higher education; second, to interrogate collectively the sources of oppression embedded in these experiences; and third, to transform a monocultural academy into one where every student's cultural identity is welcomed and honored. Throughout the project, critical thinking—the ability to analyze personal experience through critical, social analyses—becomes the means for transforming institutional policies and practices.

Origins and Development of the Critical Moments Model

At the University of Nebraska at Omaha

In the mid-1990s the Goodrich Scholarship Program at the University of Nebraska at Omaha served as an ideal incubator for Critical Moments. Established in 1972, the Goodrich Scholarship Program offers financial aid to students who demonstrate significant need; it aims to attract and retain academically able and highly motivated underrepresented students—60 percent of whom are of color and/or are first generation college students. Known for its intellectual rigor and integrated multicultural curriculum in the humanities and social sciences, the program won the 1991 Noel/Levitz Retention Excellence Award and a 2001 Hesburgh Certificate of Excellence Award.

During their first two years in the program, Goodrich students split their full-time course load between the Goodrich learning community and the university at large, earning half of their credits in each area. During their last two years, Goodrich students take courses in their majors while they continue to receive financial aid. Goodrich's unique model offers a window into students' experiences as "border crossers" on many campuses; they go back and forth between safe and unsafe places (Giroux 1992; Giroux and McLaren 1994; McLaren 1995).

In Spring 1993, when Goodrich faculty examined the transcripts from in-depth interviews with Goodrich students, they realized the validating, inclusive culture found at Goodrich had not prepared all students to deal adequately with mainstream academic culture and its often debilitating effects. Goodrich students frequently felt either *invisible* in the everyday activities of the broader university, or they felt *overly visible*, especially in public contexts where they were called on to "represent" a certain race, gender, sexual orientation, age, and/or economic class (Gillespie et al. 1996:2). These intrusive and imposed roles negated students' sense of self, and they typically "used silent negotiations to try to overcome perceived condescension and/or invisibility" (Gillespie et al. 1996:3). The interpretative frameworks that served students well in some cultural contexts proved to be unhelpful and limiting in other contexts. The disconnect between Goodrich students and the broader university further alarmed faculty who saw, in students' accounts, evidence of disengagement, the forerunner to dropping out. "We wanted," Goodrich faculty wrote, "to create spaces where students could make their silent negotiations public" (Gillespie et al. 1996:4).

The Goodrich faculty chose to create a new *curricular space*—one where students' feelings and experiences *belong* in the classroom as legitimate curriculum. With an expert facilitator, students could examine the critical moments of other students (whose identities remain anonymous), identify the broader social and cultural patterns at work, and develop proactive collaborative options for staying in school. Faculty decided to use the problem-posing approach of case-method writing and teaching to turn students' interviews into case stories steeped in students' experiences and informed by research on racial identity development and the rich literature available in multicultural education. Critical moments, though, are also an institutional matter. The first how-to guide, *Critical Moments: A Diversity Case Study Project Manual* (Gillespie et al. 1996:71), insists these moments are "critical for the university or college as the presence of cultural diversity on campus is diminished or distorted by students' silences."

With its underlying objective of reinstating student agency and transforming institutional practices, the Critical Moments model is applicable to most educational settings in which students are compelled to be border crossers, traversing the terrain between learning environments that are more or less supportive, indifferent or even hostile. As Peter McLaren (1995:142) notes, "Borders...not only demarcate otherness but stipulate the manner in which otherness is maintained and reproduced." The pilot Critical Moments Project in the Goodrich Program recognized the implications of the situational nuances in students' experiences as they moved in and out of supportive learning environments. The program aimed to increase the contributions of culturally diverse and traditionally underrepresented students, to ease their isolation, to make collaboration across cultures possible, and to promote critical reasoning and empathic understanding through the discussion of issues related to race/ethnicity, gender, class, age, sexual orientation and physical disability.

At Other Nebraska Schools

As a result of teaching cases in the Goodrich Program and implementing Critical Moments at Omaha's Metropolitan Community College and the University of Nebraska at Lincoln, a second manual, *Critical Moments: Responding Creatively to Cultural Diversity Through Case Stories*

(Gillespie and Woods 2000) introduced a fifth aim: developing diversity leadership skills among students so they can participate meaningfully in consciousness-raising activities, collectively organized across campus. This aim and the four others are now grounded in the seven-step Critical Moments model in which each step creates conditions for the next:

- Form a multicultural team to oversee the project and participate in all stages of its work.
- Identify students to interview.
- Analyze interview transcripts to identify places where students get "stuck."
- Construct case stories that embed diversity concepts in the narrative and lend themselves to rigorous analysis.
- Train facilitators in issue-oriented and critical thinking case-method discussion.
- Integrate the teaching of case studies into existing course work.
- Assess the project, especially the student learning outcomes.

Critical Moments cases are five to six pages in length. In the typical 50-minute instructional period, the facilitator/instructor introduces the case and identifies the types of skills students will practice. Having read the case beforehand, students discuss it for about 30 minutes and debrief their discussion during the remaining 15 minutes. In subsequent classes, the instructor might choose to explore issues raised in the case further by assigning supplemental materials drawn from multiple disciplines, including relevant theory, research findings, films and literature.

In Washington State

The seven steps, developed from work with three Nebraska schools, became the template for adapting and implementing Critical Moments in Washington State. The Washington Center for Improving the Quality of Undergraduate Education, a statewide consortium of two- and four-year higher education institutions housed at The Evergreen State College, coordinated the implementation of the project. From 2000 to 2004 project funding was provided by a grant from The William and Flora Hewlett Foundation. Best known for its national work on learning communities, the Washington Center also has collaborated with other campuses for over a decade and a half on a series of diversity initiatives related to inclusive pedagogy and the academic success of students of color.

Since 2000, the Washington Center and four partner institutions—Seattle Central Community College, Tacoma Community College, The Evergreen State College and South Puget Sound Community College—have implemented the Critical Moments model on their campuses (Malnarich and Gillespie 2004). Each institution drew on its long history of multicultural activism to move Critical Moments into new territory. Seattle Central Community College has developed and piloted the use of companion case stories that offer two very different and detailed perspectives on the same critical moment, one from a student's perspective and one from a faculty member's perspective. (See Gillespie, Malnarich, and Young, Forthcoming, for a more extended account of the Seattle Central project.) At both Seattle Central and Tacoma Community College, the Critical Moments teaching teams represent groundbreaking efforts to bring student affairs expertise into the classroom. The integration of Critical Moments into the work of First Peoples developed at The Evergreen State College illustrates how co-curricular activities are a fertile ground for developing student leadership and agency. At South Puget Sound Community College team members developed curriculum that used personal testimonials so students could practice empathic perspective taking. In evaluations done on all campuses, students emphasize how Critical Moments has developed their abilities to recognize and appreciate others' perspectives.

As part of the Hewlett grant, the Critical Moments teams from the four participating colleges, along with educators from other colleges and universities, met periodically to learn from one another's work. Such collaboration allowed campus teams to connect students' experiences on one campus to another. For instance, interviews on three different campuses identified the multicultural dynamics of learning math. As Sonia Nieto (1999) argues in *The Light in Their Eyes: Creating Multicultural Learning Communities*, the question "But can they do math?" is profoundly multicultural since it is about access to learning and about who is excluded from classic gatekeeper courses. Robert Moses and Charles Cobb (2001) are even more emphatic in the connection that must be drawn between learning math and students' ethnicity. In *Radical Equations: Civil Rights from Mississippi to the Algebra Project*, he maintains that the learning of mathematics (algebra, in particular) is the civil rights issue of our times since math literacy is the key to economic access. The teams' discussion of student interviews in the context of such multicultural research in mathematics led to the writing of "What's the Point?" (Malnarich and Gillespie 2004), a case that has been used in multiple contexts—classrooms, faculty development workshops and national conferences.

In another instance, some campus teams struggled with how to teach Critical Moments cases in predominantly white classrooms in ways that would avoid replicating the experience of the Hmong student who was, as she said, "put out in front of the class for a kind of display." As bell hooks (1994:43) has observed, there *is* a way to counter tokenism in predominantly white classrooms, that is, to study white privilege: "It is so important that '*whiteness*' be studied, understood, discussed—so that everyone learns that affirmation of multiculturalism, and an unbiased perspective, can and should be present whether or not people of color are present." Discussion among campus teams led to the creation of "A Very Slender Thread," a case specifically developed to address a white student's struggle with the meaning of her white privilege (Gillespie 2003). Similar to conversations around students' struggles in math courses, campus teams advanced their understanding of why teaching white privilege is fundamental to developing everyone's racial/ethnic identity. Campus teams report that the opportunity to discuss the implications of their work in depth has been one of the most rewarding aspects of the Critical Moments work in Washington State.

Successful Implementation of the Critical Moments Approach

As a result of a decade of experience on campuses in Nebraska and Washington, three essential practices have been identified, all of which are necessary for successful implementation of Critical Moments: first, the Freire-based critical pedagogy that informs case story writing and makes it different than personal testimony; second, the rationale for creating a multicultural team to shepherd and lead campus work from the project's earliest planning stages; and, third, the desirability of facilitator training if case story discussions are to foster intellectual curiosity and the habits of mind associated with able critical thinking. Each of these essential practices will be discussed in some detail below.

Freire's Generative Themes: From Personal Experience to Patterns of Inequality

The identification and analysis of generative themes anchor The Critical Moments Project, from conducting and analyzing student interviews to facilitating discussions of cases. The themes act as generators, giving energy and focus to discussions on the part of team members as they write cases and to the students as they discuss them. The term "generative theme" is taken from *Pedagogy of the Oppressed* by Paulo Freire (2002). He believed that educators must listen to and "respect the particular view of the world held by (students)" (Freire 2002:95). As they enter institutions of higher education, students bring with them ways of knowing and learning. To understand how students think, Freire (2002:96) believed that educators must investigate students' "thematic universe—the complex of their 'generative themes.'" Derived from lived experience, a generative theme is a general statement about or an assessment of reality that, upon investigation, reveals larger patterns of inequalities.

For example, take the working-class student who said to her classmates, "I really type well but don't qualify for the higher paying job at my company because I don't own a laptop computer. All the employees bring them back and forth from home." This statement is thematic; that is, based on her experiences on the job, the student has drawn a conclusion about personal resources necessary for promotion. The conclusion is generative because it points to larger economic inequities. Technology has widened the class divide. Those who are economically advantaged own home computers and other technological devices that economically disenfranchised people often cannot afford. Generative themes are a means to connect students' personal experiences to larger socioeconomic and political patterns in society. Overwhelmed by the complexities of their everyday experiences, students can become bogged down in their situations. So stuck, they are unable to formulate larger contexts for interpretation and action and often believe that they must act alone through exerting willpower. If a generative theme can be identified in their experiences, the theme will open up the situation for further thinking, investigation and even collective action. Freire argued that generative themes arise in situations that have become *limited* through socially and economically oppressive practices. Freire (2002:99) identified "limit situations" as the constellation of boundaries that constrain thoughts and actions and so prevent oppressed people from thinking and acting freely. Students must become aware of these limit situations so that they see such constraints are not immutable givens in the world but are the product of history and social relations. In the above example about laptops, what if the company did not provide them? What actions might change the policies and practices of such a company? Or what if the company did loan laptops to employees, and the student had assumed otherwise?

Critical Moments cases depict generative themes embedded in

limit situations, but case writers build in potential openings—places where protagonists could reasonably (not magically) act to change their circumstances. During discussions of the cases, students figure out where possibilities for new action might lead to different outcomes. For instance, the interview with the African American Goodrich student who hated being "the only black or one of a couple of blacks" in the classroom revealed a number of generative themes, which writers embedded in the case story "Survival Soliloquy" (Gillespie and Woods 2000).

Damien, the protagonist of this case, has lost several of his "homies," friends with whom he started college but who later dropped out. Those friends were from his neighborhood in the African American community in the town in which the college was located. During their first semester, they met between classes in the student union where they socialized. With most of those students now gone, Damien finds himself isolated; he has no real connections to academically successful students on campus. The tension between developing new friendships on campus and sticking with old friends is a generative theme. (See Tatum 1997, for the connection of this theme to racial identity development.) The case includes openings so that students can consider options for Damien. For example, in the case, an African American student leader reaches out to Damien. What might Damien learn from him? Institutionally, there is a learning center on campus but few students of color go. How could it be changed so that it is a more welcoming place for students such as Damien?

Freire believed that generative themes open discussion because the perceived limits in any situation can be otherwise arranged. Within any limit situation lie actions and interpretations that have not been considered or tested. Students often experience generative themes as double binds or paradoxes. Naming and reconsidering them stimulates new thinking and possibilities for action. What was seen as given or fixed is now open for testing and transformation. Where diversity is at issue, Critical Moments case stories give students opportunities to practice this way of thinking about limit situations.

Open discussions of generative themes related to diversity are also important for helping campus teams and students identify patterns of structural inequalities. Freire (2002:139) argued that those in power "mythicize" reality. For example, take the myth of meritocracy in the United States: students are told that their success is the result of their hard work. In part, it is, but they also need to understand the correlation between status markers such as race, class and gender and educational attainment. Such structural analyses are often new to students or only intermittently available to them. Freire noted that students experience fragments of reality in a given context; they need a structural or holistic view but often they cannot get outside their personal viewpoint. Gaining a critical understanding of reality requires disciplined, intellectual effort. What the educator must do is *present the theme* so that it stimulates critical thinking. Through interaction about the circumstances described in a particular case, students develop a bigger picture of the situation, which then allows them to generate different strategies for the protagonist and other characters in the story.

Critical Moments campus teams find that attending to generative themes determines the quality of interviews, case writing and teaching. The interviewer needs to identify a limit situation that has a vital generative theme so that the student, with the interviewer's guidance, can explore the experiential dimensions of the limit situation. Details about the student's experience are necessary for the case writer, who needs to embed the generative theme in a narrative that is believable. Both the plausibility of the case situation and its embedded generative theme create the spark for discussion among students. Finally, the facilitator of the case story discussion must be aware of the theme and plan questions in advance that will help it emerge during discussion of the case.

Critical Moments cases are not direct accounts of experience. Instead, students' experiences are coded into narratives with protagonists who face problematic situations. Embedded in these real-life stories, generative themes awaken students' thinking. Mobilized to respond, students learn to identify features of limit situations, especially those surrounding issues of race, gender, sexual orientation, class and disability. Students develop critical reasoning skills that allow them to test new possibilities in limit situations. Students experience the power of collective thinking in small groups, as opposed to an individual struggling in isolation. Ultimately students generate new options for action.

The Multicultural Team: Creating
the Institutional Conscience of the Project

A Critical Moments team needs to be culturally diverse in order to respond effectively to the critical moments of culturally diverse students. The team's diversity provides multiple perspectives on students' experiences so that the generative themes in student stories are discovered, understood and accurately depicted in case stories. Different contributors can identify biased interpretations of student interviews, locate places in the draft of a case that might promote stereotypes or help deepen how a generative theme is embedded in the case story.

The role of the Critical Moments campus team is to oversee the integrity of the project in the context of the diversity in a given setting. If Critical Moments is to take root on a campus, experience suggests that the team needs to be as culturally diverse as possible. Its membership should draw broadly from the school's community and be strategically composed so that administrators, faculty and staff are represented. Above all, the team's composition should reflect, at least minimally, the culturally diverse perspectives that will be brought out in case stories. The team also needs to garner administrative support for the project so that Critical Moments is recognized as a legitimate equity endeavor on the campus. The multicultural team is not only necessary for the success of the project with students, but it can become a powerful catalyst for creating institutional change.

The project often begins with a small group of interested faculty, administrators and staff who have read about Critical Moments or have attended training workshops. As individuals work together to explore the feasibility of the project on their campus, they gradually coalesce into a core Critical Moments team consisting of anywhere from five to 20 members. All will be actively involved in the development of the project. Each core team recruits a larger group of interested supporters who are willing to serve as specific needs arise. Early on, the team must attain human subjects approval for the project since it involves interviews with students

As the team solidifies, it needs to devote considerable attention to recruiting diverse members and educating administrators about the nature of The Critical Moments Project. Such early groundwork gains legitimacy with the campus community. This proves invaluable since a supportive administration often finds resources or bureaucratic shortcuts to help support the team and fund a coordinator (with release time) to oversee the entire process. The availability of such campus resources is fundamental, so that energy can be spent on the central activities of the project: collecting interviews, writing cases, creating curricular spaces for discussion of cases, teaching them and selecting supplemental materials.

In addition to Critical Moments being recognized as a campus-wide endeavor, teams do better work if they include faculty, staff and administrators as members. On some teams, administrators and staff become directly involved in teaching the cases; on other teams, faculty members conduct the interviews. Faculty learn about the dynamics of staff members' work with student organizations even as staff members become more aware of classroom dilemmas. Critical Moments, then, embeds learning *in community*, not just for students participating in case discussions but also for campus teams.

Case Story Facilitation: Deepening Understanding of Equity Through Critical Thinking

The primary purpose of the Critical Moments curriculum (case studies and their supplemental materials) is to foster students' critical thinking abilities and enhance their capacity to imagine new responses to diversity problems. For this reason, Critical Moments discussion groups should include 12 to 15 students, so that all participants have a chance to contribute to the discussion. Ideally, the seminar group should be composed of at least 60 percent students of color even on predominantly white campuses.

Good cases spark student discussions. Facilitators/instructors need to be trained so that these discussions become opportunities for students to practice critical thinking, an essential learning outcome of the project. Facilitators/instructors learn to be mindful about how a case might be taught by participating in campus team discussions of interview transcripts and by analyzing student responses to past efforts to teach the case.

Facilitators/instructors face two challenges: how to get students to move, during a single case discussion, from initial, one-dimensional analysis to multidimensional analysis; and, how to prepare case discussions so students systematically use their growing knowledge of diversity literature to recognize patterns of inequalities embedded in stories.

In their first experiences teaching cases, facilitators/instructors usually find that students participate readily in discussions, but their contributions tend to be disconnected. Focusing the discussion on different characters' perspectives helps students learn to recognize complexities in the case situations. Otherwise, the thread of the discussion is hard to grasp, let alone to pull through, in order to connect individual students' insights. One way to practice facilitation is to analyze videotapes of past case discussions in action. Another way is to talk with team colleagues about the case before teaching it to students.

Three phases of facilitating. Critical Moments teams have identified three distinct phases as important in facilitating a successful single case discussion. In the first phase, students are encouraged to stay focused on their understandings of the situation. By asking them to ground their remarks in the text, facilitators/instructors help students develop a sense of what is explicit and what is implicit, what they know and what they do not know about the situation. In the second phase, facilitators/instructors turn to the problem-solving skills assigned to the case, frame questions for students that encourage them to take multiple perspectives on the situation and bring to the fore the nature of the cultural diversity issues. In the third phase, facilitators/instructors invite students to consider different actions and their outcomes and to apply what they are learning to other situations.

The first phase of case discussions is particularly difficult. Facilitators face a common problem: some students simply blame the protagonist as victim. They announce that the protagonist is a loser, someone who is weak and ineffective. Their one-dimensional framing allows them to offer prescriptions: "She should just stand up to her antagonist." Such prescriptions are examples of wishful or quasi-magical thinking; that is, if the protagonist just does what we tell her to do, everything will work out. These responses seek to locate power outside the situation, as if a solution can be injected into the protagonist.

Faced with prescriptive responses, facilitators/instructors need to encourage students to see the situation from the protagonist's point of view. Students' wishes to control the situation from the outside in an authoritarian way are not surprising given the emphasis on individualism in U.S. American culture. Of course, troubles are neither located in a person or in a situation but in the interaction—really transaction—between persons and their situations. Once facilitators/instructors anticipate this type of response, they can ask questions that redirect students to the larger problematic situation and its multiple dimensions. In some instances, discussing wishful or quasi-magical thinking, as a diversity construct, can be useful. Facilitators/instructors also can emphasize how some students are not educated to think critically.

By the second phase of case discussions, students explore how cultural differences matter in the larger picture. Students often struggle to see how they fit personally in the power relations that are both in the group and in the culture at large. And, in the last phase, students apply the discussions to their lives outside the group, seeing case situations as similar to those in their own or in their friends' lives. Students figure out how they will respond proactively in situations that appear limiting. Facilitators/instructors encourage students to identify potentially supportive institutional resources, as well as individuals on campus (or in the community) who will become allies.

The need for ongoing assessment. Assessment of student learning can include a pre- and post-test measure where students write an analysis of a case story before the seminar begins and after the seminar ends. These responses can be assessed using rubrics for critical thinking, diversity appreciation and group dynamics. Videotaping early and later case discussions can reveal group process over time. In this context, students can assess their own participation in case discussions. In addition, members of a campus team should evaluate how well they are functioning, so that the team can re-orient its way of working if necessary. In general, students from the colleges implementing Critical Moments, as well as campus teams, rate the experience highly. They recommend that such a seminar be required for all students early in their undergraduate experience.

Critical Moments as a Means for Individual and Institutional Transformation

As a campuswide project, Critical Moments offers underrepresented students, especially those of color—as well as interested white students—a way to participate in dialogues about how ethnicity and race matter. As bell hooks (1994:130) says, "To engage in dialogue is one of the simplest ways we can begin as teachers, scholars, and critical thinkers to cross boundaries, the barriers that may or may not be erected by race, gender, class, professional standing, and a host of other differences." Such dialogues, anchored in student narratives, help educators and students see the transactional relationship between individual agency, larger socioeconomic patterns and collective action.

Critical theorists have noted that these larger socioeconomic patterns are not just empirical facts or characteristics of society but also are inscribed in linguistic practices, including social narratives about cultural differences that legitimize inequitable educational practices. McLaren (1995:89) argues, "If narratives give our lives meaning we need to understand what those narratives are and how they have come to exert such an influence on us and our students...We need to be able to read critically the narratives *that are already reading us*." Critical Moments gives underrepresented students a chance to look at the larger oppressive narratives that might be embedded in their stories; it also gives Critical Moments teams a chance to examine how oppressive narratives within students' stories might be mirrored in campus policies and classroom practices.

Far from being a quick diversity fix, Critical Moments requires sustained commitment on the part of many people, whether the campus community is predominantly white or diverse. Like other equity and diversity work, Critical Moments at its best is extraordinarily challenging since participants are compelled to find practical solutions to the complex, engrained patterns of disenfranchisement, entitlement and privilege that are embedded in students' stories. On predominantly white campuses, though, faculty, staff and administrators of color are typically burdened with higher education's shortcomings, along with their colleagues' expectations that *they* are best suited to "fixing" inequities within higher education. By bringing students' voices to the fore, Critical Moments attracts, over time, educators from very diverse backgrounds who share a common aspiration: that all students who enter college will be welcomed as whole people, their cultural identities and communities' histories present in the curriculum—a foundation for academic success. Critical Moments further anticipates a time when campus communities no longer render students invisible or overly visible nor remain complacent when learning environments are indifferent or hostile to students.

Sections of this chapter are taken from a recent monograph on The Critical Moments Project (Malnarich and Gillespie 2004).

114 *Ethnicity Matters*

References

Freire, Paulo. 2002. *Pedagogy of the Oppressed*. (30ᵗʰ Anniversary Ed.). New York: Continuum.

Gillespie, Diane. 2003. "The Pedagogical Value of Teaching White Privilege through a Case Study." *Teaching Sociology* 31:469–477.

Gillespie, Diane and George Woods. 2000. *Critical Moments: Responding Creatively to Cultural Diversity Through Case Stories*. 3ʳᵈ ed. Olympia, Wash.: The Washington Center for Improving the Quality of Under-graduate Education.

Gillespie, Diane, Gillies Malnarich, and Tina Young. Forthcoming. "Critical Moments: A Case-Based Diversity Project that Engages and Enlivens Campus-Wide Efforts to Teach and Work Inclusively." In *Teaching Inclusively: Diversity and Faculty Development*, edited by M. L. Ouellett. Stillwater, Okla.: New Forums Press.

Gillespie, Diane, Jeannette Seaberry, and Joseph A. Valades. 1997. "From Student Narratives to Case Studies: Diversity from the Bottom up." *Journal of Excellence in College Teaching* 7:25–42.

Gillespie, Diane, Jerry Cederblom, Jeannette Seaberry, Joseph Valades, and Judith Harrington. 1996. *Critical Moments: A Diversity Case Study Project Manual*. Omaha: The Goodrich Scholarship Program, University of Nebraska at Omaha.

Giroux, Henry. 1992. *Border Crossings: Cultural Workers and the Politics of Education*. New York: Routledge.

Giroux, Henry and Peter McLaren, eds. 1994. *Between Borders: Pedagogy and the Politics of Cultural Studies*. New York: Routledge.

Hansen, Daryl and Diane Gillespie. 1998. "Struggles in the Classroom: A Deaf Student's Case." *Journal of College Reading and Learning* 28:132–136.

Henning, Denise and Diane Gillespie. 1996. "The First Amendment: A Case Study." *The National Teaching & Learning Forum* 5(5):4–5.

hooks, bell. 1994. *Teaching to Transgress: Education as the Practice of Freedom*. New York: Routledge.

Malnarich, Gillies and Diane Gillespie, eds. 2004. *The Critical Moments Project*. Olympia, Wash.: The Washington Center for Improving the Quality of Undergraduate Education.

McLaren, Peter. 1995. *Critical Pedagogy and Predatory Culture*. New York: Routledge.

Moses, Robert and Charles E. Cobb. 2001. *Radical Equations: Civil Rights from Mississippi to the Algebra Project*. Boston: Beacon Press.

Nieto, Sonia. 1999. *The Light in Their Eyes: Creating Multicultural Learning Communities.* New York: Teachers College Press.

Seaberry, Jeannette. 1994. "Familial and Environmental Factors Shaping the Experiences of a Black Male Collegian: A Qualitative Inquiry." Ph.D. dissertation, College of Education, University of Nebraska, Lincoln, Neb.

Seaberry, Jeannette and Diane Gillespie. 1997. "The White Teacher." *National Teaching & Learning Forum* 6(3):11–12.

Tatum, Beverly D. 1997. *"Why Are all the Black Kids Sitting Together in the Cafeteria?" and Other Conversations about Race.* New York: Basic Books.

Valades, Joseph A. 1994. "Chicano Perceptions of Self and School: A Symbolic Interactionist Study." Ph.D. dissertation, College of Education, University of Nebraska, Lincoln, Neb.

———. 1996. "Misunderstood." *National Teaching & Learning Forum* 6(1):8–9.

6

How and Why Ethnicity Matters: A Model for Developing Programs That Serve Students of Color

MaryJo Benton Lee

The four previous chapters describe, in considerable detail, innovative programs that are highly effective in preparing students from underrepresented groups for college and in supporting these students through baccalaureate degree completion. These programs are both innovative and effective because they are built on the proposition that *ethnic identity can play an empowering role in academic achievement*. The authors of the four previous chapters present an enormous body of information about the workings of their particular programs. Certainly, readers need to understand what works and why in these programs, but that alone is not sufficient. Readers also need to know how to replicate the successes described in the programs they themselves currently run or in programs they hope to create. That is the aim of this chapter. Chapter Six parallels Chapter One in that it addresses both *theoretical* and *practical* concerns.

Chapter Six begins with *theoretical* concerns. Earlier models of minority college student preparation and retention are presented first.

Next, a new theoretical model, depicting how college preparation and retention programs help students of color succeed, is proposed. One purpose of the new theoretical model is to simplify the complex, that is, to take the myriad facts presented on program creation, planning, implementation and evaluation in Chapters Two through Five, and achieve some generality useful to others tackling issues of minority underrepresentation in higher education. Another purpose of the new model is to explain the essential mechanisms that make the programs described in this book innovative, effective—and worth emulating.

The new theoretical model answers the three key *Ethnicity Matters* questions posed in Chapter One: Does a strong ethnic identity empower students of color to achieve academically? Why do students who have strong ethnic identities tend to do well in school? And, how could this knowledge be used to foster academic success for students of color?

"One of the major criticisms of critical theory is that individuals cannot often envision what abstract ideas look like when they are employed," William Tierney (2000:214) writes. The four programs described in this book are all examples of critical race theory put into practice.

Thus, it is fitting that Chapter Six ends with *practical* concerns. Using "community cultural wealth" (Yosso 2005), which will be explained in detail later, is the key to designing effective programs for students of color. A summary of the very best practices from all four of the Ethnicity Matters programs described earlier in the book is contained in Chapter Six. Clustered under the headings of familial, social, aspirational, linguistic, navigational and resistant capital, readers can find a menu of activities to select from for use in their own work with students of color.

The chapter concludes with ten overarching principles that emerge from the texts of the chapter authors. These are ideals that guide all of the Ethnicity Matters programs and make them the exemplars they are today. A final section addresses the need for hope on the part of those to whom ethnicity matters.

Earlier Models of Minority College Student Preparation and Retention

Vincent Tinto's Longitudinal Model of Institutional Departure (Tinto 1993:114) is the most highly acclaimed model that attempts to explain why some students depart from college. As discussed in detail in Chapter One, numerous scholars question the validity of the Tinto model to adequately describe the experiences of nonwhite students. Some of these scholars propose alternative models.

For example, the work of Watson Swail focuses on *retaining* minority students in higher education. Swail (2003:88) points out that "most frameworks or 'models' focus on departure and the paths through post-secondary education," while his Model of Minority Student Persistence and Achievement focuses on student retention and success. Swail's framework "provides administrators and practitioners with a menu of activities, policies, and practices to consider during the planning and implementation of a comprehensive campus-based retention program" (Swail 2003:90).

William Tierney (2000:226–227) puts forth another alternative to Tinto with his Culturally Responsive Model for Educational Success. "The model I am trying to develop works from the idea that those individuals who have been labeled 'at-risk' or are likely to drop out have much greater potential than previous frameworks suggest," Tierney writes (2000:223).

G. Arthur Jackson (2003:131), in a book titled *Saving the Other Two-Thirds: Practices and Strategies for Improving the Retention and Graduation of African American Students in Predominantly White Institutions* (Jackson 2003:131), presents a Campus-Inclusion Model with ten steps for "reducing attrition and enhancing retention by putting the components of the educational community together."

The models just described (Swail 2003; Tierney 2000; Jackson 2003) all focus on minority student *retention*, not on minority student *departure* (Tinto 1993). The Swail, Tierney and Jackson models are largely *conceptual*, in that they are composed of patterns of interrelated concepts, not expressed in mathematical form and not primarily concerned with quantification (Theodorson and Theodorson 1969:261–262). These models are *macro*-theoretical, in that they deal with minority student preparation and retention at the institutional level.

It is important to note that there are other models that are *mathematical* and that operate at the *micro*-level. They illustrate the strength of the relationship between racial-ethnic identity and school achievement among individual elementary, middle school, high school and university students. These models are also *causal* in that the development of "ethnic identity" (Oyserman, Gant, and Ager 1995; Taylor et al. 1994) and "racial-ethnic attitudes" (Smith, Atkins, and Connell 2003) are seen as preceding and affecting academic achievement.

A New Theoretical Model: Understanding How Students of Color Succeed

The title of this book promises a "rethinking" of how black, Hispanic and Indian students prepare for and succeed in college. Thus, the model developed here will depart somewhat from the others described previously. That said, the work of Daphna Oyserman and William Tierney, discussed above and at length in Chapter One, have been immensely influential in the development of the new model.

Understanding How Students of Color Succeed

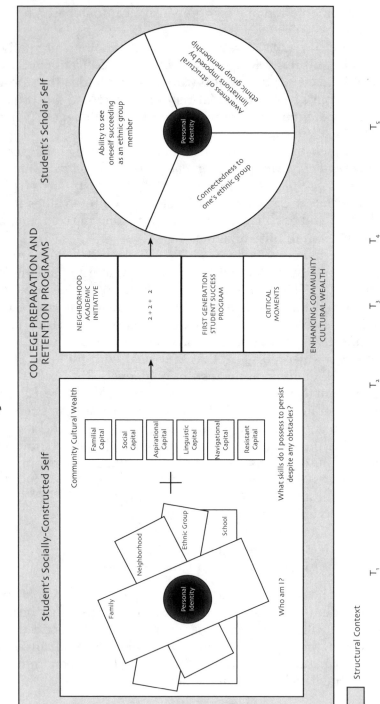

The new model is causal and conceptual. The model operates at the micro-level in that it deals with identity construction processes occurring before entry into high school and at the end of college (in T_1 and T_5). Micro-level processes are described in lower case letters. The model also operates at the macro-level in that it looks at how effective college preparation and retention programs enhance the community cultural wealth that students bring with them into school (T_2, T_3 and T_4). Macro-level processes are described in upper case letters.

Student's Socially Constructed Self

A model is a simplification of reality, created in the interest of achieving generality (Jary and Jary 1991:312). The social construction of self is an immensely complex process. (For a more detailed description of the construction of self see Lee 2001:72–73). The model presented here looks at only two aspects of the process, as experienced by successful students of color in the pursuit of higher education. These are *personal identity* and *community cultural wealth*.

Personal identity. A student constructs a personal identity by comparing his or her own definition of self with that of significant others (Heiss 1981). In this case, significant others are people with whom the student interacts in the family, neighborhood, ethnic group and school, people to whom the student orients him- or herself while moving through the early phases of the life cycle. Contradictions inevitably arise between how the student defines him- or herself and how others see the student. Thus, the answer to the key personal identity question "Who am I?" is arrived at jointly, in a social context.

For a black, Hispanic or Indian student, developing a personal identity involves assembling a positive sense of self while discrediting negative identities generally attributed to students of color (Oyserman, Gant, and Ager 1995). A student's ethnic identity schema (a set of organized generalizations about the self) has a profound effect on how the student fares academically. Conversely, a student's ethnic identity schema is profoundly affected by experiences the student has in school.

Community cultural wealth (versus traditional cultural capital). All minority college preparation and retention programs aim to supply students of color with the necessary capital to succeed within the system as it presently exists (Tierney 2000:217). Pierre Bourdieu's notions of capital—economic, social and cultural—were discussed in detail in Chapter Two. *Economic capital* often takes the form of generous scholarships, like the ones supplied by the First Generation Student Success Program (FGSSP). *Social capital* is at work when students are linked to existing support networks on campus, for example, when 2+2+2 helps its participants develop personal relationships with campus resource people who then become vested in American Indian student success.

Bourdieu (1977, 1986) defines *cultural capital* as a collection of knowledge, skills and abilities possessed and inherited by privileged groups in society. Cultural capital is acquired from one's family or through formal schooling. Dominant groups maintain their power by limiting access to cultural capital itself and by limiting opportunities for learning how to use this capital to achieve upward social mobility (Yosso 2005:76). Cultural capital, once narrowly regarded as a resource inherited from one's family or acquired through formal schooling, is now regarded as a set of skills that can be taught by state-sponsored sources (Mehan et al. 1996:216). So when the Neighborhood Academic Initiative (NAI) helps participants fill out college applications, find tutors and use the library, it is providing cultural capital to those whose family members and neighborhood schools may not be able to do so.

Bourdieu's ideas about capital and its importance in educational attainment have had an immense impact on those working toward educational equity. It is important to note, however, that Bourdieu's ideas place value on a very narrow range of assets (Yosso 2005:76). Tara Yosso (2005), writing from a critical race theory perspective, explains the problems that Bourdieu's ideas create for students of color and for those who work with them:

> His theory of cultural capital has been used to assert that some communities are culturally wealthy while others are culturally poor. This interpretation of Bourdieu exposes White, middle class culture as the standard, and therefore all other forms and expressions of 'culture' are judged in comparison to this 'norm.' In other words, cultural capital is not just inherited or possessed by the middle class, but rather it refers to an accumulation of specific forms of knowledge, skills and abilities that are *valued* by privileged groups in society. (P. 76)

So the question becomes how to reconcile Bourdieu's useful explanation for social reproduction with a healthy respect for Communities of Color and for the resources they provide to nurture their students. Tierney's answer is that those working with minority high school and college students must develop culturally responsive programs "whereby students hold on to and affirm their own embedded identities while they function and succeed within the received culture of multiple kinds of educational institutions at the turn of the century" (Tierney 2000:218). The four programs described in this book operate from Tierney's position that students traditionally labeled "at risk" are actually valuable resources to themselves and to their families, communities and society (Tierney 2000:222). As well, even though these students come from families without college degrees, they have an immense amount of "community cultural wealth" (Yosso 2005:78) upon which to draw, a resource that their more formally educated teachers may not possess.

The focus for Bourdieu is on students' resources. The focus for Tierney and Yosso is on students *as* resources.

Yosso (2005:77) defines "community cultural wealth" as the accumulated assets and resources derived from the histories and lives of African American, Hispanic American and American Indian communities. Students of color inherit their "community cultural wealth" from their families, neighborhoods, ethnic groups and, in some cases, from their local schools. Put another way, "community cultural wealth" is "an array of knowledge, skills, abilities and contacts possessed and utilized by Communities of Color to survive and resist macro and micro-forms of oppression" (Yosso 2005:77).

Yosso's concept of "community cultural wealth" (Yosso 2005) is similar to Ann Swidler's notion of culture as a "tool kit" (Swidler 1986:273). Culture provides an individual with a "tool kit" of skills from which to construct strategies of action. The "tool kit" may include symbols, stories, rituals and worldviews, derived from membership in a particular ethnic group, that an individual uses, in varying configurations, to solve different kinds of problems.

The six ideal types of capital that constitute "community cultural wealth" (Yosso 2005:77–81) are described below, using Yosso's words:

- "Familial capital" refers to those cultural knowledges nurtured among kin that carry a sense of community history, memory and cultural intuition.
- "Social capital" can be understood as networks of people and community resources that can provide both instrumental and emotional support to navigate through society's institutions.
- "Aspirational capital" refers to the ability to maintain hopes and dreams for the future, even in the face of real and perceived barriers.
- "Linguistic capital" includes the intellectual and social skills

attained through communication experiences in more than one language and/or style.
• "Navigational capital" refers to skills of maneuvering through social institutions not created with Communities of Color in mind.
• "Resistant capital" refers to those knowledges and skills fostered through oppositional behavior that challenges inequality.

Structural Context

Adolescence has often been viewed as a time of unfettered identity negotiation, when youths try on various roles, convey self-conceptions to others and receive feedback (Oyserman, Gant, and Ager 1995:1216). It is important to remember, however, that social structures influence self-conceptions. Certain structural factors such as class, status and power may constrain interaction. As Sheldon Stryker (1989:53) writes, "Constraints...may exist within situations with respect to the behavioral expression of given identities...One cannot be a swimmer in the absence of a pool."

A successful student of color must develop a personal identity that allows him or her to persist within the larger structural context, a context that often limits the occupational, educational and economic attainment of minorities (Ogbu 1978, 1985, 1992). In addition, a successful student of color must be able to overcome "stereotype threat", that is, others' judgments that minority group membership means lowered academic achievement (Steele 1997).

While personal identity and community cultural wealth are certainly most important, many other variables are involved in the social construction of self for the student of color. The shading in the model, which indicates structural context, is intended to remind readers of this.

College Preparation and Retention Programs

Ethnicity Matters—deeply—in Neighborhood Academic Initiative, 2+2+2, First Generation Student Success Program and Critical Moments. The concept of community cultural wealth (Yosso 2005) is useful in explaining how these programs make ethnicity central to academic success. The four Ethnicity Matters programs require students of color to use the community cultural wealth they bring with them to school. In addition, the programs deliberately seek to enhance the students' community cultural wealth, so that it further empowers them to succeed in school. Exactly how this works will be discussed later in this chapter, after the model has been fully explained.

It is important to note here, however, that for both students of color and for white students, the salience of ethnicity varies. Individuals are free agents. Personal identity construction can be viewed as choosing cards from a deck. At one moment an individual may choose the "female" card, at another moment the "African American" card, and at yet another, the "married" card. It is possible for two students of color, who grew up in the same community and maybe even in the same family, to experience varying degrees of attachment to their ethnic group.

The Ethnicity Matters programs use and reinforce students' community cultural wealth, to the extent that the students bring this wealth to school with them. The Ethnicity Matters programs also generate community cultural wealth for those students of color who do not already possess it. That will also be discussed later in the chapter.

Critical Junctures in Time

Increasing the number of students of color who earn bachelor's degrees requires attention to four critical junctures: academic preparation in high school, graduation from high school, enrollment in college and college persistence to degree completion (Swail 2003:11). Viewed as a group, the Ethnicity Matters programs have a remarkable record of meeting students at and sustaining students through each of these critical junctures.

As discussed earlier, the passage of time through high school and college coincides with a time of identity negotiation for youth. They try on different identities, relaying self-conceptions and receiving feedback from others ranging from family and neighbors to peers and teachers. As Daphna Oyserman, Larry Gant and Joel Ager (1995:1216) explain, "In this way youths synthesize childhood identities with what they know of their skills and abilities and construct adult selves that are at once plausible and at least reasonably satisfying."

Student's Scholar Self

Effective programs, like the ones described in this book, are designed to create definitions of the situation that assume success for students of color (Tierney 2000:225). In order for a student to succeed academically, a "scholar self" must evolve over time as a result of a series of negotiations and reconstructions of personal identity (Hodges and

Welch 2003:2). This identity work occurs both inside and outside of school. Put another way, developing a "scholar self" means developing an ability to see academic achievement as *possible*, even in a structural context strewn with systemic racial and ethnic barriers.

The odds against college persistence to degree completion are staggering for the student of color. Only 41 percent of American Indians and African Americans who start college actually finish. The percentage of Hispanics who finish college is 49 percent (Harvey 2003:23). It is known that youths are more likely to invest effort in endeavors they believe they can complete successfully (Oyserman, Harrison, and Bybee 2001:384). "Perceived efficacy" means believing one has the power to influence one's environment and control one's destiny. A sense of efficacy can bolster adolescent resilience and academic achievement, leading to persistence in school (Oyserman, Harrison, and Bybee 2001:379).

Oyserman and colleagues, as part of an ongoing research program, are exploring three components of ethnic identity that seem related to perceived efficacy (Oyserman, Gant, and Ager 1995; Oyserman, Harrison, and Bybee 2001). They are:

- connectedness to one's ethnic group;
- ability to see oneself succeeding as an ethnic group member; and
- awareness of structural limitations imposed by ethnic group membership.

Conceptualizing oneself as a group member and developing a view of oneself succeeding as a group member, as well as becoming aware of stereotypes and other limitations, are all outcomes of participation in the programs described in this book—three final examples of how ethnicity matters in successful minority college preparation and retention efforts.

How Model Answers Key *Ethnicity Matters* Questions

This book began by posing three key questions. These questions will now be revisited, in light of the book's findings and in light of the model developed to explain the findings. The questions are:

- Does a strong ethnic identity empower students of color to achieve academically?
- If so, why do students who have strong ethnic identities tend to do well in school?

- Furthermore, how could this knowledge be used to foster academic success for students of color?

Does a Strong Ethnic Identity Empower
Students of Color to Achieve Academically?

The minority college preparation and retention programs described in this book are all highly successful. They have proven track records, developed over many years, of helping students of color prepare for and succeed in college. Their success rate sets them apart from many other programs with the same aims. The programs described in this book are unique in that they make ethnicity central to success. Thus, it seems fair to say that a strong ethnic identity can empower many students to achieve academically.

Why Do Students Who Have Strong Ethnic Identities
Tend to Do Well in School?

An answer is again provided by the model programs studied. These programs do not treat students of color as deficient because they enter school lacking the necessary cultural capital to persist. Rather, these programs recognize that students of color often come to school with huge amounts of cultural wealth, acquired from the Communities of Color where they were raised. The Ethnicity Matters programs actively work to multiply these students' assets—familial, social, aspirational, linguistic, navigational and resistant capital. In short, these programs both use and strengthen ethnic identity.

As a result, students served by these programs are able to construct *scholar selves*. These students see themselves as being connected *to* their ethnic groups and see themselves succeeding *as* members of their ethnic groups. These students consistently view success as *possible*, even when facing structural barriers like prejudice and discrimination. In short, the ability to see oneself as a successful *African American* scholar, a successful *Latino/a* scholar or a successful *American Indian* scholar is fundamental to academic achievement.

How Could This Knowledge Be Used to Foster
Academic Success for Students of Color?

By looking carefully at how the four model programs use and multiply various forms of community cultural wealth, readers will better understand how to work with minority students as they prepare for and succeed in college. The remainder of the book will address this matter in some detail. At this point the text shifts from the theoretical to the practical.

The next section will review the best practices of each of the four Ethnicity Matters programs. These practices will be organized around the six types of community cultural wealth already discussed. Readers can use the next section much like a menu, picking and choosing activities from the Ethnicity Matters programs for use in their own work with students of color.

Using Community Cultural Wealth: The Key to Effective Programs for Students of Color

Community cultural wealth is the scaffolding that supports the four model programs featured in this book. Community cultural wealth is "the array of cultural knowledge, skills, abilities and contacts possessed by socially marginalized groups that often go unrecognized and unacknowledged" (Yosso 2005:69). Community cultural wealth means the assets that many students acquire from Communities of Color and bring with them to school. Each of the Ethnicity Matters programs draws on this community cultural wealth (to the extent that it exists in the population served) to ensure that students persist in school to degree completion. The programs sometimes create community cultural wealth, where it is lacking, in order to foster student success.

Community cultural wealth can be conceptualized as six types of capital frequently possessed by students of color: familial, social, aspirational, linguistic, navigational and resistant. Each type will be discussed in detail below, with examples drawn from the Ethnicity Matters programs.

Familial Capital

Familial capital is "those cultural knowledges nurtured among...kin that carry a sense of community history, memory and cultural intuition" (Yosso 2005:79). In this context, "kin" is defined broadly and includes nuclear and extended family members—siblings, parents, aunts, uncles and grandparents—both living and dead. "Kin" for students of color may also include legal guardians, people to whom they may or may not be related by blood. Since students of color often move into and out of higher education at various stages in the life cycle, spouses and children also are key members of their kinship systems.

An extensive body of knowledge is evolving around the notion of "familial capital." For example, Douglas Foley (1997:118–119) points to African American families, who while they may not match the middle-class ideal of the two-parent nuclear family, are clearly strengthened by their reliance on traditional African norms of reciprocity and extended kinship. Educational ethnographer Concha Delgado-Gaitan (2001:53) describes how Latino/a families are able to "transcend oppressive difficulties and find their sources of strength and power" needed to reform community schools.

First Generation Student Success Program. Using familial capital is key to all of the Ethnicity Matters programs, but none more so than the FGSSP at the University of La Verne (ULV). It is a retention program specifically designed to help students *and families* overcome obstacles and get degrees. A large percentage of these students and families are Latino/a. Working with students' families begins during the first visit to campus. Understanding parental perceptions of students' needs, staff point out the smallness of the campus, the personal attention from faculty and the closeness to home to assure families that ULV is a good fit for their children.

As prospective students transition to college, FGSSP makes sure that their families are involved every step of the way. FGSSP provides money for transportation, hotels and meals, allowing families to accompany students to campus. Orientation is planned with both students and their families in mind. Orientation workshops focus on topics like academic self-confidence, which is often lacking in first generation college students and students of color.

ULV's research shows that family is a primary motivation for Latino/a students. Recognizing the sacrifices made on their behalf, students express a desire to fulfill the expectations of their families for success, first in college and later in careers. Consequently, FGSSP creates a family team of supporters, all committed to that student's success. Family members are given ULV T-shirts and other university memorabilia to take home with them, further cementing the bonds between themselves and ULV.

Neighborhood Academic Initiative. NAI prepares families of color, emotionally and financially, to send their children off to college. NAI creates partnerships with families, investing in students' futures and sharing in their successes. Parents and guardians must engage in the following activities in order for their children to be program participants:

- Encourage children to study at home.
- Notify NAI when children are having problems outside of school.
- Attend one parent-oriented NAI session each month.
- Volunteer to assist NAI staff with one program per year.
- Serve on one NAI family committee.

Active inclusion of family ensures that NAI alumni fulfill both the promise of the program and the dreams of their families.

2+2+2. Another family-friendly program, 2+2+2 serves many Native American students who are themselves parents. Free child care and preschool tuition waivers allow nontraditional 2+2+2 students to attend classes at South Dakota State University (SDSU), students who might otherwise not enroll. In addition, travel funds allow family members to travel to the SDSU campus to support 2+2+2 students whenever important—on initial visits, when homesickness strikes or for graduation ceremonies.

Social Capital

Social capital is "networks of people and community resources...(that) provide both instrumental and emotional support to navigate through society's institutions" (Yosso 2005:79). Historically, people of color have used their social capital to obtain education, employment, health care and legal justice for themselves, and then have reinvested these resources back into their social networks (Yosso 2005:79–80). This tradition is well illustrated by the "Lifting as I rise" motto of the National Association of Colored Women's Clubs (Guinier, Fine, and Balin 1997:167).

Neighborhood Academic Initiative. "Neighborhood" is an integral part of NAI's success. "Neighborhood" for NAI is the living laboratory in the front yard of the University of Southern California (USC), where the program is headquartered. Students are not removed from their primarily African American and Latino/a communities in order to become NAI Scholars. Rather, NAI shapes itself to meet local needs. USC, the Los Angeles Unified School District and two local high schools all act as good neighbors to each other, pooling their resources to achieve community well-being.

NAI actively works to maintain a culture of collaboration and inclusion:

• *Community members* are essential components of the learning process, mentoring NAI Scholars and presenting Saturday programs.
• *Teachers and counselors* for NAI are often from local communities and underrepresented groups.
• *Students* themselves are encouraged to help each other with assignments and to mentor other community youth.
• *Alumni* of the program are called on to share their stories of inspiration with the next generation of NAI Scholars.

2+2+2. Most Native American students served by 2+2+2 come from reservation communities geographically far removed from SDSU. For 2+2+2, using the social capital of the students served means keeping the program connected to Native American communities and tying SDSU personnel into networks of Native American people. These are tremendous challenges.

The program overcomes these challenges by making money available to staff and students for frequent travel between reservation high schools, tribal colleges and SDSU. Non-Indian faculty working in the 2+2+2 program clearly realize the importance of traveling to reservation communities, to learn literally where their Indian students are "coming from."

Because face-to-face interaction is not always possible, the 2+2+2 program also makes money available to ensure robust communication among partner institutions. Personal correspondence, e-mails, newsletters and a Web site are all key tools used by 2+2+2. American Indian culture places a high value on listening carefully, committing to action and following through. Consequently, good communication, despite geographical barriers, is fundamental.

For 2+2+2, relying on the social capital that students bring with them into the program means respecting the knowledge created within tribal communities. It is important to note that the inspiration for 2+2+2 came from tribal college staff. Their primary goal was to help more American Indian students complete baccalaureate degrees and return to reservation communities prepared to meet the challenges facing Native people today.

The project continues to operate as a partnership among equals at three types of institutions—reservation high schools, tribal colleges and a state university. Native people work as planners, promoters and implementers of 2+2+2 programming, designed to serve Native students. Planning retreats are frequently held on Indian reservations and facilitated by tribal educators.

Each "two" of 2+2+2 is an example of using the social capital generated by Native American communities to support Indian students as
they navigate through high school and college. The program meets students where they are, that is, in their local high schools on the reservations. When these students come to SDSU for their first 2+2+2 programs,
personnel from their high schools, many of them Native people, serve
as teachers and staff. Programming for high school students attending
2+2+2 summer institutes at SDSU includes preparing Native foods,
playing hand games and making star quilts. Students learn about the
past from tribal elders and use "talking circles" to discuss contemporary issues. Clearly the social capital of Native communities is not only
respected in 2+2+2 , but is a centerpiece of the program's operation.

After high school, 2+2+2 students move on to tribal colleges,
starting higher education in their own reservation communities. The
mission of the tribal colleges is to explore, rebuild and reinforce American Indian culture using curricula and settings conducive to Native
students' success. Tribal colleges are believed to strengthen students'
ethnic identity, which may, in turn, help students who transition to
predominantly white institutions to complete degrees. Articulation
agreements, transfer guides, course-by-course equivalencies and coordinated course offerings between the tribal colleges and SDSU all
ensure that work completed at the tribal colleges will be accepted by
SDSU. Put another way, the knowledge generated by Indian scholars in
Indian classrooms is valued by SDSU, the predominantly white institution where students will finish their degrees.

Reliance on the social capital of American Indians is also evident in
the third "two" of 2+2+2, that is, at SDSU. University faculty members
work hard to integrate Native American perspectives into courses that
the 2+2+2 scholars and other students take. Substantial grants allow
professors to travel to reservations, hear Native speakers, buy necessary books—in short, to become more culturally competent teachers.
Faculty from SDSU and tribal colleges are now teaching collaboratively.
Technology, such as interactive television and Internet courses, helps
break down barriers to successful collaboration. These changes benefit
both Indian and non-Indian students.

First Generation Student Success Program. FGSSP is unique among the
Ethnicity Matters programs in that it is "data driven." FGSSP began
with an extensive study of first generation college students at ULV. The
study revealed the obstacles faced by this largely Latino/a and largely
female population. Generally speaking at ULV, first generation students

come from lower income families and have poorer GPAs and SATs than other students. The first generation students often live off campus with family and work while attending school. The initial study led administrators to design a retention effort, FGSSP, which relies on some important social capital that many first generation ULV students bring to school with them. This social capital is the strength of the traditional Latino/a family. All FGSSP programming aims to support students and families as they *together* move through the college experience.

Aspirational Capital

Aspirational capital is "the ability to maintain hopes and dreams for the future, even in the face of real and perceived barriers" (Yosso 2005:77). The phrase *"esperar contra toda esperanza"* (to hope against all hope) has been used to describe the resiliency of Latino/a transnationals, who under the most adverse circumstances, function effectively on both sides of the Mexican border (Trueba 1999:xxxviii). Miguel Guajardo and Francisco Guajardo (2002) further illustrate the meaning of aspirational capital with the following example:

> The pitiful indicators would suggest that our students (at Edcouch-Elsa High School in the Rio Grande Valley) would be dropping out of school, working in the fields, and standing on the welfare lines. But ask our sixty students—all Mexican American, all poor (meaning working class)—who have gained acceptance into Ivy League universities since 1993, when we began to dream and imagine that a kid like Delia Perez, whose father worked in the fields and whose mother was a housewife, could go to a place like Yale University…After Yale, Delia returned to Edcouch-Elsa to teach and has since enrolled at the LBJ School of Public Affairs. (Pp. 287–288)

Yosso (2005:78) and others explain aspirational capital as a culture of possibility that breaks the links between parents' current occupational status and children's future educational attainment.

2+2+2. The program began on South Dakota's Indian reservations with high school and tribal college faculty, students, and community leaders sharing their hopes and dreams for the new endeavor. This is significant in terms of aspirational capital because the inspiration for 2+2+2 came from Native people who continue to suffer from a traumatic legacy, including economic, educational, cultural and spiritual oppression.

The goal of 2+2+2 is to develop resident expertise among American Indians on South Dakota reservations, enabling tribal people to become better prepared to meet some of the most serious challenges facing them today. The initial dream of the 2+2+2 organizers—to prepare tribal people for career areas of critical need to Indian communities—is being realized today, ten years later.

The 2+2+2 program builds on the aspirational capital of American Indians who are already academically and professionally successful. The importance of American Indian role models in 2+2+2 cannot be overemphasized. Prominent tribal leaders deliver keynote addresses. Native faculty and staff at SDSU are an integral part of the program, presenting workshops and advising students. Indian students and alumni of the university also work as counselors in the program, sharing their own stories of challenge and success.

The 2+2+2 project also generates aspirational capital within its participants. Experiential learning, like research apprenticeships and summer institutes, motivates students to pursue higher education and professional careers. The hands-on approach of 2+2+2 encourages students to try on different professional American Indian identities, for example, "I can be a Native American dietician." The program fosters career awareness in a culturally relevant context. Summer institute workshops may range from Native American cultural symbolism in interior design to Geographic Information Systems applications on Indian reservations.

All 2+2+2 programming emphasizes that a strong American Indian ethnic identity is linked to academic achievement. The American Indian students participating in the program are constantly defined and redefined as successful. First, they complete applications to be considered for the program. Next, the students, their families and their schools receive congratulatory letters of acceptance into the program. The central message is that the students have become part of a select group of Native American scholars. This image is reinforced throughout their time in the program via pictures and text on 2+2+2 brochures, traveling displays and the Web site. Award ceremonies and honoring programs also affirm student success. Scholars proudly wear their 2+2+2 T-shirts. New releases to the media in Indian communities recognize students' accomplishments.

Across all cultures, spirituality keeps aspiration alive in seemingly hopeless circumstances. "Life is full of hardships, difficulties and unpredictable events, yet the communication of a religious and cultural message of peace and confidence renews the energy of many to keep trying," says Enrique (Henry) T. Trueba (2002). In 2+2+2, gatherings begin and conclude with traditional Lakota prayers. Students often "smudge" with smoke from burning sage to ask for the creator's guidance. Sweat lodge ceremonies are held for 2+2+2 students in conjunction with important milestones.

First Generation Student Success Program. New student and family orientation is an opportunity for FGSSP students and their relatives to discuss, at the start of school, what they want out of college and what it will take to fulfill these aspirations. Many Latino/a students at ULV are the first in their families to attend college. These students, families and peer mentors gather periodically throughout the school year to celebrate milestones along the path to achieving these goals. Awards are given to dean's list students, top mentors and parent volunteers.

Neighborhood Academic Initiative. NAI uses the label "Scholar" to refer to its participants, helping them aspire to be successful high school students and future college-goers. NAI emphasizes that academic achievement is a characteristic that cuts across all ethnic groups. NAI's goal is to develop *African American* Scholars and *Latino/a* Scholars.

"I like coming here…you know, you get to be at college while you're still at high school," one NAI Scholar said. The aspirations of the NAI Scholars are affirmed by the experience of taking classes on the USC campus. The Scholars have a chance to see themselves in university classrooms, mastering college-level work.

Linguistic Capital

Linguistic capital is "the intellectual and social skills attained through communication experiences in more than one language and/or style" (Yosso 2005:78). Bilingual students bring with them to school a lifetime of experience translating for their parents in diverse settings ranging from banks and government agencies to movies and doctors' offices. As a result, these students develop a complex set of abilities that may actually help them do better in school than their monolingual peers. These abilities include "vocabulary, audience awareness, cross-cultural awareness…metalinguistic awareness (ability to reflect on language), teaching and tutoring skills, civic and familial responsibility, (and) social maturity" (Orellana 2003:6).

Both the First Generation Student Success Program at the University of La Verne and the Neighborhood Academic Initiative at the University of Southern California involve large numbers of students whose native language is Spanish. These programs respect and use the linguistic capital of the Spanish-speaking students they serve and, by extension, the linguistic capital of these students' families.

First Generation Student Success Program. Accommodations for Spanish-speaking parents involved in FGSSP are numerous. These accommodations include making sure that materials delivered to students' homes are linguistically appropriate and providing Spanish-speaking counselors to work with parents during all workshops. In addition, each family is assigned a personal contact at the university, someone who will be available to answer questions whenever they arise.

Neighborhood Academic Initiative. NAI conducts its Saturday parent sessions in Spanish and in English. Organizers explain that this accommodation invites parents into the educational process and validates their importance in the program. Session topics range from strategies for effective parenting to creating study space at home.

Navigational Capital

Navigational capital is the skill of "maneuvering through social institutions...not created with Communities of Color in mind" (Yosso 2005:80). Dealing every day with systems permeated by racism, people of color learn not only how to survive, but how to thrive. Trueba (2004:162), writing about immigrants in cross-cultural settings, says that the most resilient individuals are those who are able "to use multiple identities and to understand the strategic value of playing different roles, using different languages, controlling communicative skills in sending messages to different audiences, and manipulating information from different possible frameworks of interpretation." John Ogbu (1992:12) describes the navigational skills of successful students of color as "accommodation without assimilation." "When in Rome, do as the Romans do, without becoming Romans," Ogbu advises.

Neighborhood Academic Initiative. NAI students, many of them African American and Latino/a, routinely navigate through the problems associated with growing up in the low-income, urban area of south central Los Angeles. These students cope daily with problems ranging from drugs and gangs to unemployment and violence—and still manage to be serious scholars. NAI supports students in this process by providing counseling to address the social and emotional issues associated with adolescence.

First Generation Student Success Program. Most Latino/a students who participate in FGSSP have a lifetime of experience navigating through social institutions not created with people of color in mind.

Certainly higher education is one of those institutions. FGSSP reinforces the navigational strengths that Latino/a students bring with them into the program by linking each student with a trained mentor. These mentors are drawn from a variety of groups, such as alumni, faculty, staff and junior/senior minority students, at ULV. Students and mentors together develop "growth plans," identifying possible majors, assessing career interests and planning navigational strategies to cope with the challenges of being a first generation college student. Through the mentoring program, students learn about university resources that will reinforce the navigational capital they bring with them to school.

2+2+2. Seeing one's culture reflected in the day-to-day operations of a predominantly white university is a tremendous navigational aid for students of color trying to negotiate their way to degree completion. Support from numerous campus entities has enhanced SDSU's Native American literature and art collections and has sponsored Native American speakers and entertainers. An American Indian History and Culture Conference and a *Wacipi* (pow-wow) have become annual events that draw hundreds of Native and non-Native people to campus. Ongoing faculty development efforts are aimed at topics such as Native American learning styles. SDSU also continually tries to strengthen the academic advising of Native American students and to incorporate more American Indian perspectives into courses across the curriculum.

Native Americans constitute almost 10 percent of South Dakota's population, thus Native American students in South Dakota have vast experience in navigating through institutions not created with people of color in mind. The 2+2+2 program reinforces the navigational capital of its Indian students by helping them get to know Native American Club members, the Native American student adviser and other Native American students and faculty across campus. Through culturally sensitive orientation activities, incoming students are tied into existing support systems. Culturally sensitive support systems are now in place at SDSU to help Native students deal with problem situations that may differ significantly from those of non-Native students. These culturally sensitive support systems include free tutoring for all Native American students, an emergency fund for unexpected financial crises, help finding housing that will accommodate families and assistance dealing with the Indian Health Service.

Critical Moments. Critical Moments is a diversity case-story project designed to foster critical thinking skills. Critical Moments begins with the premise that most college students of color must navigate through predominantly white institutions that routinely expect them to leave their cultural identity outside the classroom door. Critical Moments makes *all* its students more aware of the socially and economically oppressive practices that exist on campuses and in communities.

Critical Moments reinforces the existing navigational capital of students of color by developing their diversity leadership skills and by identifying supportive institutional resources. In addition, Critical Moments teaches students of color and white students how to collaborate across cultures and work toward academic success for all.

Resistant Capital

Resistant capital is "those knowledges and skills fostered through oppositional behavior that challenges inequality" (Yosso 2005:80). A rich body of scholarship, spanning multiple cultures and time periods, has developed around the notion of resistant capital. Vine Deloria Jr. (1969) writes about "the intangible unity" that has carried American Indians through four centuries of persecution. Paulo Freire (2002) describes the transformative power of education, which allowed once illiterate peasants in Brazil to take on the very structures of the society that oppressed them. Henry Giroux (1983:293) puts his hope in contemporary American schools to create "pockets of resistance…in the struggle for a new morality."

Neighborhood Academic Initiative. NAI acknowledges that racism exists and is a very real challenge for the black and Hispanic students from south central Los Angeles who the program serves. NAI teachers, many of them black and Hispanic, remind students that their job is to figure out ways to overcome discrimination and to attend college. Students are not allowed to blame racism for poor academic performance.

NAI's aim is to eradicate racist tendencies in all students. "Derisive language, stereotyping, and ethnic grouping of black students versus Hispanic students are vigorously rejected in favor of an approach that accentuates pride in one's heritage and respect for others," writes Tierney (2000:229), who has studied NAI extensively.

2+2+2. The 2+2+2 program also acknowledges the very real presence of racism in the everyday lives of Native American students at SDSU. The program hosts sessions on confronting racism for both SDSU faculty and residence hall staff. Participants in 2+2+2 hear panel discussions by Native American alumni, discussing the discrimination they have faced and strategies for coping with it. These strategies include developing support networks and using campus services like the counseling center and the Native American student adviser.

Throughout its history, the 2+2+2 program also has aggressively pursued institutional change. Articulation agreements, initially developed for 2+2+2, now make it easier for all students to move back and forth between tribal colleges and SDSU. Faculty across campus work more effectively with Native students as a result of training received through 2+2+2. The 2+2+2 summer institute has become an annual, SDSU-sponsored event. Indeed, an entire new constellation of projects, benefiting American Indian students across campus, presently exists ten years after 2+2+2 began. These projects include TRiO Student Support Services, Upward Bound, a minority recruiter, a Native American nursing program, an Office for Diversity Enhancement, the SDSU-Flandreau Indian School Success Academy, a graduate cohort program for tribal college faculty, and numerous collaborative SDSU/tribal college research projects.

Critical Moments. Critical Moments identifies patterns of inequality on campus. Through the discussion of diversity case stories, students, faculty and staff become aware of oppressive policies and practices. Individuals see how they personally fit into the power relations of the university and of the culture at large. Critical Moments makes visible experiences of underrepresented students and collectively interrogates the sources of oppression.

Critical Moments actively works to transform monocultural institutions into places where every student's cultural identity is honored. The project creates a new "curricular space," in the words of its organizers, where the experiences of students of color belong in the classroom as legitimate curriculum. This, in turn, diversifies the education for all students on campus.

The multicultural teams of case writers and facilitators have become catalysts for creating institutional change on the campuses that have adopted Critical Moments. These people—faculty, staff and administrators—see the diversity dilemmas in each other's work. Together they are able to reform indifferent and hostile learning environments. Educators of color, who have typically been charged with "fixing" inequities on campus, now share this task with white colleagues.

Making Ethnicity Matter: Ten Principles
That Guide Effective Programs

"One must understand that critical pedagogy is not only about theoretical ideas, " writes Barry Kanpol (1994:175). "It is also about living those ideas in our daily lives in and out of our workplace." Sharing our stories is crucial because in this way we teach each other what is possible.

This book is a sharing of stories. The chapter authors have shared with readers their accomplishments—and sometimes their frustrations—in designing programs for students of color, programs in which ethnicity truly matters. The previous section of this chapter contained a "to-do list" of Ethnicity Matters activities, compiled for readers who wish to create similar successful programs at their own institutions. It is important to remember, however, that the whole is more than the sum of its parts. There are threads of meaning, which tie the Ethnicity Matters stories together and give them life. Thus, in this final section of the book, I will try to capture some of the unifying principles that all of the successful programs share—and that the rest of us should recognize—as we attempt to make ethnicity matter in our own workplaces and in our daily lives.

Since all good programs are contextually situated, the first three principles deal with time, and the next two principles deal with space. No discussion of ethnicity could be complete without some discussion of power and privilege, and those two sociological concepts are addressed in principles six through eight and in principle nine, respectively. The tenth principle addresses the critical need for research in program design, implementation and evaluation.

Timing is everything. The organizers of effective programs are keenly aware of when the timing is right for systemic change. Tim Nichols and Laurie Stenberg Nichols attribute, in part, the successful launching of 2+2+2 to "fortuitous timing." Reservation highs schools were eager to see more of their students attend college. Tribal colleges were hoping to have a larger share of their students complete associate degrees and eventually baccalaureate degrees. SDSU was emphasizing diversity and recruiting more Native American students.

Similarly, the FGSSP was born out of some race-related incidents at ULV, negative responses by minorities on a student satisfaction survey and a campus population that was growing more ethnically diverse. These factors caused the La Verne administration to take a more proactive stance toward university diversity, and one positive outcome was FGSSP.

In short, cogent advice to would-be project planners is this: Be keenly aware of the political climate at your institution and take advantage of opportune moments as soon as they arise.

"Early" and " intensive" describe the best programs. NAI begins preparing its students for college when they start seventh grade. Students attend accelerated English and math classes at USC for two hours at the start of every school day. A Saturday Enrichment Academy and summer school courses round out the program. Students of color, like those in NAI, are heirs to a centuries-long legacy of racial discrimination and unequal access. Modest interventions and quick "fixes" do not begin to level the playing field. Only through sustained and intensive effort will educational equity be achieved.

Persistence is the key. It is important for universities to keep the long-term perspective in mind and not expect to see minority student enrollment jump overnight. As 2+2+2 creators Nichols and Nichols (1998:41) observe, "This persistence is in keeping with Lakota philosophy, which considers not only what is good for today and tomorrow but also what will be good for seven generations into the future." This is but one of many important lessons that white mainstream Americans can learn from Native Americans.

Wherever you are, be there. Geography is of the essence. In the NAI, the emphasis is on "neighborhood." The students served come from communities whose front yards adjoin the USC campus. It is here students take their classes, taught by local teachers, supported by family members.

The 2+2+2 program involves partners in reservation communities and at SDSU, separated by hundreds of miles. Considerable time and money have been invested to provide transportation between institutions, so that faculty can collaborate face to face and students can move easily between schools.

Sometimes "being there," in a geographical sense, can be achieved quite simply. In the FGSSP, participants receive their scholarship checks directly from the FGSSP director. This ensures that students enter the FGSSP office space regularly and receive all the support they need.

Good communication is the next best thing to being there. Those who work in successful programs spend an extraordinary amount of effort keeping in touch with one another. Besides correspondence and e-mail, 2+2+2 uses a Web site, regular newsletters, press releases, traveling displays and program brochures to communicate with project partners and the general public. Courses are shared between 2+2+2 member institutions using interactive television and the Internet.

Julia Colyar, writing about NAI, points out the importance of programs generating their own success stories. These success stories then become the subject matter of local and national news reports that, in turn, may attract even more supporters.

It pays to have (or cultivate) friends in high places. The importance of having people in power backing programs that benefit students of color cannot be underestimated. This was the one factor mentioned by all the chapter authors as contributing to their projects' success.

Supportive administrators at SDSU and at other partner institutions removed structural barriers and provided the moral and financial support for the 2+2+2 program to get under way. NAI began under the auspices of the office of the provost at USC, an office that holds distinction and suggests a weight of commitment.

FGSSP grew, in part, out of a campuswide diversity task force, appointed by ULV President Stephen C. Morgan. The task force was composed of students, faculty and staff from throughout the university, but it is important to note that all the academic deans, student affairs deans, the academic vice president and the president himself were also members.

Writers Diane Gillespie, Gillies Malnarich and George Woods, reflecting on the implementation of the Critical Moments project on campuses across the country, say that "garnering administrative support" is fundamental. Programs that benefit students of color and the institutions they attend must be recognized as legitimate equity endeavors. This happens only when support comes from those with power.

Collaboration works. A willingness to share power—between individuals, among institutions and, most importantly, across races—benefits both the more powerful and the once powerless.

The 2+2+2 creators point out that the initial request for collaboration came from American Indian people. Tribal college staff came to SDSU seeking a partnership program that would help more of their students complete baccalaureate degrees. The end result was 2+2+2, an educational ladder with every rung in place, which allows students to smoothly transition from reservation high school to tribal college to SDSU.

The success of NAI also rests on the "collaborative relations of power" (Tierney 2000:219) that develop among students, families, communities and NAI staff. Involving parents, guardians, community leaders and neighborhood mentors in NAI conveys respect for the knowledge and strength that these people bring to the college preparatory process.

Critical mass counts. Universities are viewed as the foundations of democracy, responsible for opening the doors of social participation to *all* peoples—especially those who have been oppressed (Trueba and Zou 1994:218). The rhetoric of openness, however, often stands in stark contrast to the practice of restricted acceptance for ethnic minorities. Embedded power structures permit individuals from dominant groups to retain control of higher education—and to retain control of all subsequent opportunities open to those with college degrees.

Logically, the percentage of students of color admitted to any university—and graduated by that university—should approximate the percentage of people of color in the general population served by that university. The legacy of educational and economic oppression, suffered by people of color throughout American history, makes this a challenging goal. Nevertheless, the best minority college preparation and retention programs are those that strive, in their daily practice, to meet this standard, in the long run. ULV, where the FGSSP operates, has an exemplary record. ULV's 32 percent Latino/a enrollment mirrors the 32 percent Latino/a population of the state of California.

Put another way, outstanding programs that serve students of color routinely work toward achieving "critical mass." "Critical mass" means having enough students around who are like oneself so as not to feel isolated, uncomfortable and alone (Astone and Nunez-Wormack 1990:65). Critical Moments authors Gillespie, Malnarich and Woods explain that, in the absence of critical mass, students of color feel either *invisible* in the everyday activities of the broader university or they feel *overly visible*, especially in public contexts where they are called on to "represent" a certain race.

Money matters. Privilege is defined as possession or control of a portion of the surplus produced by society. Sociologist Gerhard Lenski (1984:45) notes that "privilege is largely a function of power, and to a very limited degree, a function of altruism."

Most programs serving students of color begin with funding from external grants, funding that the universities are expected to assume, once the grants expire. Those few programs that do survive beyond the expiration of their initial grants are those that have the backing of powerful people. Powerful people are those who control a significant share of the resources at their institutions and can, when they choose, direct these resources toward programs that benefit ethnic minorities.

The best example, from the projects discussed, is FGSSP. When the initial, three-year $500,000 grant expired, the ULV president found $100,000 per year in ULV's general budget to continue the program. That allocation, together with a new scholarship endowment awarded to ULV from the Packard Foundation, has kept FGSSP going strong ten years after its creation.

USC continues to provide a great deal of in-kind and material support to NAI. Similarly, as the 2+2+2 program has matured, more responsibility for ongoing financial support has been absorbed by the project partners—SDSU, five tribal colleges and 15 reservation high schools. A university's commitment to diversity may well be judged by the willingness of its leaders to invest in the education of students of color.

Data drive great projects. This is the tenth and final principle that the Ethnicity Matters programs can teach and that we can learn. ULV conducted a three-year research project to better understand and remove some of the obstacles faced by first generation college students, especially those who are also members of minority groups (Reisberg 1999: A43). ULV then used the experiences reported by respondents to design FGSSP. Len Hightower, an author of the FGSSP chapter and a former administrator at ULV, explains the rationale behind this plan: "We wanted a data-driven program, based on the needs and expectations of those we're trying to serve, not the typical program, which is based on the ideas of administrators and faculty members" (Reisberg 1999: A43). Listening to those the program intends to serve is a hallmark of all the Ethnicity Matters programs. In FGSSP, continuous improvement assessment, involving both students and parents, helps staff monitor program progress and make necessary improvements.

The Audacity of Hope

Hope is the final principle that unites those to whom ethnicity matters. We teach in public schools burdened by the demands of No Child Left Behind, an underfunded mandate that identifies unsatisfactory performance without developing any measures to correct the problems

(Atwell 2004). We work in universities beset by a "testing mania," where excellence is supposedly measured by the test scores of entering students (largely white), rather than by the retention of all students. Looking beyond our local schools, we find barriers to participation in education worsening nationwide. There is a move away from need-based student aid, a rise in public university tuition and vociferous attacks on affirmative action. In the face of such disturbing trends, only the "audacity of hope" (Barack 2004) unifies us and energizes us to make ethnicity matter for our schools, for our students and for ourselves.

Paulo Freire, the author of a book titled *Pedagogy of Hope*, spent a lifetime bringing literacy to the oppressed in Brazil—and was rewarded with exile by his country. Freire (1992) writes:

> Hope is an ontological need. Hopelessness is but hope that has lost its bearings, and become a distortion of that ontological need...Hopes, as it happens, is so important for our existence, individual and social, that we must take every care not to experience it in a mistaken form, and thereby allow it to slip toward hopelessness and despair. Hopelessness and despair are both the consequence and the cause of inaction or immobilism...One of the tasks of the progressive educator, through a serious, correct political analysis, is to unveil opportunities for hope, no matter what the obstacles may be. (Pp. 8–9)

Freire became the teacher of Enrique (Henry) T. Trueba. The two met in 1984, when Henry was teaching at the University of California, Santa Barbara. Henry later visited Freire in Brazil and came to regard Freire as his "spiritual and intellectual leader" (Trueba 2004:x). As Henry explains, "Influenced by Paulo Freire...I began to deconstruct my previous experiences" (Trueba 2004:xvi). Those experiences ranged from Henry's ministry as a Jesuit to rural villagers in Mexico to his work as an educator among immigrant populations in the United States.

Henry came to South Dakota State University in the fall of 2002 to give the keynote address at our Ethnicity Matters conference. Throughout the two-day event, his wisdom, his humor and his fire energized and inspired all those present. Henry made the journey to Brookings, South Dakota, from Houston, Texas, where he was undergoing treatment for cancer. Weakened in body, but not in spirit, Henry and I debated for weeks by phone, letter and e-mail whether he was strong enough to make the trip. He did, and by so doing, he became the teacher of all of us who created this book and who now dedicate it to his memory. We cherish these words he wrote to us after the conference:

> There are so many types of friendship and so many experiences, no? But to get to know you in your setting,...in your institution was an extraordinary

opportunity. In a very unexpected...way we discovered each other... and gradually realized that we had in common...a profound commitment to intellectual work, a full engagement into scholarly work directed to action research, and a serious decision to impact the lives of the young...All of a sudden, many of those principles and commitments joined us together and gave us a chance to share our lives...Realizing how much more we had in common, I came back to Texas fully aware that the Lord had planned this trip for me from the very beginning. So I have been and will always be totally grateful. (Trueba 2003)

As a teacher, researcher, author and scholar, Henry traveled the world, working tirelessly to create learning opportunities for those in greatest need. He frequently used metaphors relating to travel, like this one, to remind us of our highest calling:

A pedagogy of hope does not exist in a cultural vacuum. Entering someone else's culture is somewhat comparable to the immigration experience without the risks and the mourning that immigrants have to suffer...The praxis that accompanies a pedagogy of hope is clearly a conscious detachment from "whiteness" and from a rigid, dogmatic, and monolithic defense of a Western or North American way of life, schooling codes, and interactional patterns...Educators who are serious about their praxis and committed to a pedagogy of hope must be prepared to take a long and hazardous psychological trip into lands and minds unknown before. (Trueba 1999:160–161)

We will always be totally grateful that our paths crossed Henry's on one of his many journeys. His passion to better understand and improve education for students of color lives on in our own work. Ethnicity *does* matter—and that is what keeps hope alive.

References

Astone, Barbara and Elsa Nunez-Wormack. 1990. *Pursuing Diversity: Recruiting College Minority Students.* Washington, D.C.: School of Education and Human Development, George Washington University.

Atwell, Robert H. 2004. "The Long Road Ahead: Barriers to Minority Participation Persist." Pp. 1–3 in *Reflections on 20 Years of Minorities in Higher Education and the ACE Annual Status Report.* Washington, D.C.: American Council on Education.

Barack, Obama. 2004. Speech at Democratic National Convention, 27 July, Boston Fleet Center, Boston, Mass.

Bourdieu, Pierre. 1977. "Cultural Reproduction and Social Reproduction." Pp. 487–511 in *Power and Ideology in Education,* edited by J. Karabel and A. H. Halsey. New York: Oxford University Press.

———. 1986. "The Forms of Capital." Pp. 241–258 in *Handbook of Theory and Research for the Sociology of Education,* edited by J. G. Richardson. New York: Greenwood Press.

Delgado-Gaitan, Concha. 2001. *The Power of Community: Mobilizing for Family and Schooling.* Lanham, Md.: Rowman & Littlefield Publishers.

Deloria Jr., Vine. 1969. *Custer Died for Your Sins: An Indian Manifesto.* New York: Avon Books.

Foley, Douglas E. 1997. "Deficit Thinking Models Based on Culture: The Anthropological Protest." Pp. 113–131 in *The Evolution of Deficit Thinking: Educational Thought and Practice,* edited by R. R. Valencia. Washington, D.C.: The Falmer Press.

Freire, Paulo. 1992. *Pedagogy of Hope.* New York: Continuum.

———. 2002. *Pedagogy of the Oppressed.* (30th Anniversary Ed.). New York: Continuum.

Giroux, Henry A. 1983. "Theories of Reproduction and Resistance in the New Sociology of Education: A Critical Analysis." *Harvard Educational Review* 53:257–293.

Guajardo, Miguel A. and Francisco J. Guajardo. 2002. "Critical Ethnography and Community Change." Pp. 281–304 in *Ethnography and Schools: Qualitative Approaches to the Study of Education,* edited by Y. Zou and H. T. Trueba. Lanham, Md.: Rowman & Littlefield Publishers.

Guinier, Lani, Michelle Fine, and Jane Balin. 1997. *Becoming Gentlemen: Women, Law School, and Institutional Change.* Boston: Beacon Press.

Harvey, William B. 2003. *20th Anniversary Minorities in Higher Education Annual Status Report.* Washington, D.C.: American Council on Education.

Heiss, Jerold. 1981. *The Social Psychology of Interaction.* Englewood Cliffs, N.J.: Prentice-Hall.

Hodges, Carolyn R. and Olga M. Welch. 2003. *Making Schools Work: Negotiating Educational Meaning and Transforming the Margins.* New York: Peter Lang.

Jackson, G. Arthur. 2003. *Saving the Other Two-Thirds: Practices and Strategies for Improving the Retention and Graduation of African American Students in Predominantly White Institutions.* Ames, Iowa: Jackson Challenge Fund and Associates, Iowa State University.

Jary, David and Julia Jary. 1991. *The HarperCollins Dictionary of Sociology.* New York: HarperCollins Publishers.

Kanpol, Barry. 1994. *Critical Pedagogy: An Introduction.* Westport, Conn.: Bergin & Garvey.

Lee, MaryJo Benton. 2001. *Ethnicity, Education and Empowerment: How Minority Students in Southwest China Construct Identities.* Burlington, Vt.: Ashgate.

Lenski, Gerhard E. 1984. *Power and Privilege: A Theory of Social Stratification.* Chapel Hill: The University of North Carolina Press.

Mehan, Hugh, Irene Villanueva, Lea Hubbard, and Angela Lintz. 1996. *Constructing School Success: The Consequences of Untracking Low-Achieving Students.* New York: Cambridge University Press.

Nichols, Laurie Stenberg and Tim Nichols. 1998. "2+2+2: Collaborating to Enhance Educational Opportunities for Native Americans." *Journal of Family and Consumer Sciences* 90:38–41.

Ogbu, John U. 1978. *Minority Education and Caste.* New York: Academic Press.

———. 1985. "Research Currents: Cultural-Ecological Influences on Minority School Learning." *Language Arts* 62:860–869.

———. 1992. "Understanding Cultural Diversity and Learning." *Educational Researcher* 21(8):5–24.

Orellana, Marjorie Faulstich. 2003. *In Other Words: Learning From Bilingual Kids' Translating and Interpreting Experiences.* Evanston, Ill.: School of Education and Social Policy, Northwestern University.

Oyserman, Daphna, Kathy Harrison, and Deborah Bybee. 2001. "Can Racial Identity Be Promotive of Academic Efficacy?" *International Journal of Behavioral Development* 25:379–385.

Oyserman, Daphna, Larry Gant, and Joel Ager. 1995. "A Socially Contextualized Model of African American Identity: Possible Selves and School Persistence." *Journal of Personality and Social Psychology* 69:1216–1232.

Reisberg, Leo. 1999. To help Latino students, a college looks to parents. *The Chronicle of Higher Education.* 15 January, A43–A44.

Smith, Emilie Phillips, Jacqueline Atkins, and Christian M. Connell. 2003. "Family, School, and Community Factors and Relationships to Racial-Ethnic Attitudes and Academic Achievement." *American Journal of Community Psychology* 32:159–173.

Steele, Claude M. 1997. "A Threat in the Air: How Stereotypes Shape Intellectual Identity and Performance." *American Psychologist* 52:613–629.

Stryker, Sheldon. 1989. "Further Developments in Identity Theory: Singularity Versus Multiplicity of Self." Pp. 35–57 in *Sociological Theories in Progress: New Formulations*, edited by J. Berger, M. Zelditch Jr., and B. Anderson. Newbury Park, Calif.: Sage Publications.

Swail, Watson Scott. 2003. *Retaining Minority Students in Higher Education: A Framework for Success*. San Francisco: Wiley Periodicals.

Swidler, Ann. 1986. "Culture in Action: Symbols and Strategies." *American Sociological Review* 51:273–286.

Taylor, Ronald D., Robin Casten, Susanne M. Flickinger, Debra Roberts, and Cecil D. Fulmore. 1994. "Explaining the School Performance of African-American Adolescents." *Journal of Research on Adolescence* 4:21–44.

Theodorson, George A. and Achilles G. Theodorson. 1969. *A Modern Dictionary of Sociology*. New York: Barnes & Noble Books.

Tierney, William G. 2000. "Power, Identity and the Dilemma of College Student Departure." Pp. 213–234 in *Rethinking the Student Departure Puzzle*, edited by J. M. Braxton. Nashville: Vanderbilt University Press.

Tinto, Vincent. 1993. *Leaving College: Rethinking the Causes and Cures of Student Attrition*. Chicago: The University of Chicago Press.

Trueba, Enrique (Henry) T. 1999. *Latinos Unidos: From Cultural Diversity to the Politics of Solidarity*. Lanham, Md.: Rowman & Littlefield Publishers.

———. 2002. "Resilience and Ethnicity." Keynote speech at Ethnicity Matters conference, 18 October, South Dakota State University, Brookings, S.D.

———, Ruben E. Hinojosa Regents Professor (Emeritus), University of Texas, Austin. 2003. Correspondence with author, 5 November, Houston, Texas.

———. 2004. *The New Americans: Immigrants and Transnationals at Work*. Lanham, Md.: Rowman & Littlefield Publishers.

Trueba, Henry T. and Yali Zou. 1994. *Power in Education: The Case of Miao University Students and its Significance for American Culture*. Washington, D.C.: The Falmer Press.

Yosso, Tara J. 2005. "Whose Culture Has Capital? A Critical Race Theory Discussion of Community Cultural Wealth." *Race Ethnicity and Education* 8:69–91.

Contributors

Julia E. Colyar completed her Ph.D. in higher education policy and organization at the University of Southern California (USC). While at the Center for Higher Education Policy Analysis at USC, she was involved in a national Ford Foundation study pertaining to the effectiveness of college preparation programs for low-income urban youth. She is currently an assistant professor of Educational Administration and Higher Education at Southern Illinois University Carbondale, where she teaches courses in equity and diversity, college student development, and qualitative methods. Her research interests include access and retention for historically underrepresented students in higher education, innovations in qualitative methodology and writing, and the intersections of fiction and social research.

Diane Gillespie, professor and associate director of Interdisciplinary Arts and Sciences (IAS) at The University of Washington, Bothell, received her Ph.D. in 1982 at the University of Nebraska at Lincoln in cultural and psychological studies in education. In IAS, she teaches multicultural social science courses and qualitative research. She has won seven different awards for her teaching, including the 1992 Nebraska CASE Professor of the Year Award. Her recent publications explore the importance of narrative for reflective teaching and learning. She helped pilot and develop The Critical Moments Project at the University of Nebraska at Omaha. Since 1998, she served as consultant to The Washington Center for Improving the Quality of Undergraduate Education as the Center helped nine colleges in Washington State implement The Critical Moments Project.

Len Hightower received his bachelor of arts in psychology from Westmont College, master's in social science from Azusa Pacific University and Ph.D. in education from the Claremont Graduate University. While serving as the executive assistant to the president, he originated and wrote the initial program and grant for the First Generation Student Success Program at the University of La Verne in Southern California. He also served as the chair of the University of La Verne task force on diversity for a decade. He has more than 25 years of experience in higher education, and he currently serves as the vice president for enrollment management and director of strategic planning at Pacific University in Oregon.

MaryJo Benton Lee holds bachelor's and master's degrees in journalism from the University of Maryland-College Park. She worked for five years as a newspaper reporter in the Washington, D.C., area, covering issues ranging from urban hunger to teen pregnancy. She holds a Ph.D. in sociology, with a minor in Asian studies, from South Dakota State University (SDSU). During her 20 years at SDSU she has held a number of positions, both teaching and administrative, most recently that of diversity coordinator for the College of Engineering. She is also the co-founder and the coordinator of the SDSU-Flandreau Indian School Success Academy, an early and intensive college preparatory program. She is an adjunct assistant professor in the University of South Dakota's School of Education. She has been an exchange professor and visiting scholar at Yunnan Normal University, People's Republic of China. Her first book was Ethnicity, Education and Empowerment: How Minority Students in Southwest China Construct Identities (Ashgate 2001).

Gillies Malnarich co-directs The Washington Center for Improving the Quality of Undergraduate Education at The Evergreen State College. Educated in the humanities and social sciences, she has taught both in higher education (at universities, a four-year college and a large urban community college) and out of higher education (in workplaces, women's centers, community-based schools and other adult education programs). She has worked with educators on abilities-based teaching, learning, assessment and institutional effectiveness. At the Washington Center, she works to support campuses by focusing on the design of integrated curricula and assignments, learning communities, equity issues, and preparing students for demanding college-level work.

Laurie Stenberg Nichols received her bachelor of science degree in home economics education from South Dakota State University, master of science in vocational and adult education from Colorado State University, and Ph.D. in family and consumer sciences education/family studies from Ohio State University. For two years she was a faculty member at Wayne State College in Nebraska and for six years at the University of Idaho, where she received numerous teaching and research awards. In 1994 she returned to her alma mater to become dean of the College of Family and Consumer Sciences. She has secured numerous grants to collaborate with South Dakota tribal colleges in the areas of nutrition and early childhood education.

Tim Nichols earned his bachelor's in agriculture and master's in adult and continuing education from Washington State University, along with a Ph.D. in sociology from South Dakota State University (SDSU). He currently works as assistant director of academic programs in SDSU's College of Agriculture and Biological Sciences. In addition to coordinating student services and faculty development, he has been an impetus for expanding outreach to tribal colleges and American Indian communities in South Dakota, attracting more than $1 million in extramural funding to support these efforts.

Enrique (Henry) T. Trueba was born in Mexico in October 1931, the tenth child in a family of 12 children. As a Jesuit, he worked for many years serving rural villagers in Mexico. He received a master's in anthropology from Stanford University and a Ph.D. in anthropology from the University of Pittsburgh. His career as an educational anthropologist included professorial and administrative assignments at multiple universities. He served as dean of the School of Education at the University of Wisconsin, Madison, and as senior vice president for academic affairs and provost at the University of Houston. In 2001 he retired from the College of Education at the University of Texas, Austin, where he held the rank of Ruben E. Hinojosa Regents Professor. The following academic year he taught in the doctoral program of the University of Texas, Pan American. At the time of his death in July 2004, he was a visiting scholar at Rice University. He was the author of 24 books focused on ethnicity, education and empowerment of minorities. His research consistently centered around issues of identity, adaptation and learning among immigrant populations. He received countless fellowships, honors and awards, including being named a member of the National Academy of Education.

Derek Vergara was the executive director of the Institute for Multicultural Research and Campus Diversity, Office of the President, at the University of La Verne in Southern California. As co-founder of the institute, he developed and facilitated universitywide diversity research and program initiatives dealing with faculty course transformation, campus-community partnerships with local African American churches, and first generation college students. He received a bachelor's degree in social work and a master's degree in social sciences from Azusa Pacific University. He is pursuing a doctorate in education at the University of La Verne. He has worked in higher education for 20 years, including time at the University of La Verne; University of California, Riverside; University of California, Irvine; and Pepperdine University. He is currently serving as a consultant for Advance Infant Development, designing an autism spectrum disorder program for infants.

George Woods, M.D., is a neuropsychiatrist, board certified by the American Board of Psychiatry and Neurology. He graduated from Westminster College, Salt Lake City, and the University of Utah Medical Center. He is currently on the faculties of Morehouse School of Medicine in the Department of Psychiatry and California State University, Sacramento, in the Department of Educational Leadership and Public Policy. He also has taught at The University of Washington, Bothell. He is consultant to The Critical Moments Project at The Washington Center for Improving the Quality of Undergraduate Education.

Index

Bernal, M., 15, 18
Bergin, D., 11
Black Man's Think Tank, 25
blocked opportunities, 9, 10, 18
Bond, M., 69
bonding, 73
Bonous-Hammarth, M., 46
Bourdieu, P., 7, 49, 50, 73, 121, 123
Boyer, P., 58, 59
bridging, 73
bridging capital, 73
Bridging the Achievement Gap, 19
Brookings Institute, 19
Brown v. Board of Education, 1
Buenavista, T. L., 26
Bull, C. C., 65
Bybee, D., 16, 126

-C-

Campus-Inclusion Model, 119
Cantu, C. L., 67
Carter, C., 58
Center for Academic Support, 42
Central Institute for Nationalities, 12
Chapell, M. S., 10
Chen, X., 40
Chubb, J., 19
Cobb, C., 104
Colyar, J., 47, 48, 142
community cultural wealth, 118, 121,
   123, 124, 128
Connell, C. M., 119
conscientization, 13, 23
Cooks, H., 11
Cooper, D. L., 11
Cooper, R., 13
Cooperative Institutional Research
   Program, 88
Critical Moments, 3, 5, 19, 29, 31, 99–
101, 112–13, 124, 137–38, 139, 142
   case story facilitation at, 110–12
   implementation of, 105–108
   in Washington State, 103–105
   multicultural team at, 108–110
   origins and development of, 101–
      102

*Critical Moments: A Diversity Case
   Study Project Manual*, 102
*Critical Moments: Responding
   Creatively to Cultural Diversity
   Through Case Stories*, 102
critical pedagogy, 7–8
cultural
   capital, 49–51, 73, 122
   differences, 9
   ecological theory, 9, 10
   integrity, 51–52
   knowledge, 49
Culturally Responsive Model for
   Educational Success, 119
curricular space, 139

-D-

Datnow, A., 11
Delgado-Gaitan, C., 129
Deloria, V. Jr., 138
Design for Diversity, 25
Deyhle, D., 18, 51
disidentification, 52
Dodson, N. E., 15
Dukes, R. L., 67
Dumont, R., Jr., 58
Durkheim, E., 7

-E-

economic capital, 122
efficacy, 16
Escamilla, K., 14
Escuela Tlatelolco, 22
ethnic identity, 3, 118
   academic identity and, 14, 117, 127
   definition of, 14
   minority students and, 11–12
   school performance and, 9, 12, 13–
      18
*Ethnicity, Education and
   Empowerment*, 28, 29
ethnic minorities
   academic failure, 11
   access to college, 19–27
   bias towards, xiii
   campus climates and, 24
   college attendance and, 2

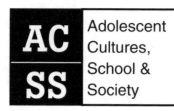

Adolescent
Cultures,
School &
Society

Joseph L. DeVitis & Linda Irwin-DeVitis
GENERAL EDITORS

As schools struggle to redefine and restructure themselves, they need to be cognizant of the new realities of adolescents. Thus, this series of monographs and textbooks is committed to depicting the variety of adolescent cultures that exist in today's post-industrial societies. It is intended to be a primarily qualitative research, practice, and policy series devoted to contextual interpretation and analysis that encompasses a broad range of interdisciplinary critique. In addition, this series will seek to provide a pragmatic, pro-active response to the current backlash of conservatism that continues to dominate political discourse, practice, and policy. This series seeks to address issues of curriculum theory and practice; multicultural education; aggression and violence; the media and arts; school dropouts; homeless and runaway youth; alienated youth; at-risk adolescent populations; family structures and parental involvement; and race, ethnicity, class, and gender studies.

Send proposals and manuscripts to the general editors at:

Joseph L. DeVitis & Linda Irwin-DeVitis
The John H. Lounsbury School of Education
Georgia College & State University
Campus Box 70
Milledgeville, GA 31061-0490

To order other books in this series, please contact our Customer Service Department at:

(800) 770-LANG (within the U.S.)
(212) 647-7706 (outside the U.S.)
(212) 647-7707 FAX

or browse online by series at:

WWW.PETERLANG.COM